How To Self-Publish a Children's Book

YVONNE JONES

Publisher: LHC Publishing

ISBN-10: 0997025492
ISBN-13: 978-0997025491

Printed in the U.S.A.

DEDICATION

To all aspiring children's book authors...

DOWNLOAD THE ACCOMPANYING TEMPLATES & SWIPE FILES WE'LL BE USING IN THIS BOOK.

TO DOWNLOAD, GO TO:

http://www.eevijones.com/book-downloads

EESCRIBE

"Whatever you can do (or dream you can), begin it. Boldness has genius, power and magic in it."

~ Johann Wolfgang von Goethe

You're busy.
It can be hard to find time to follow your dreams. But you won't need long stretches of time to write your children's book. It's all about how you make use of the little time you do have.

You only need to begin in order to succeed. And I'll show you how!

I've created a short video (mp3 also available), to help you find little pockets of time you can use to implement all that you'll learn in this book.

Watch the FREE VIDEO now, and say "YES" to becoming a children's book author:

http://www.eevijones.com/make-time-write-childrens-book

CONTENTS

ACKNOWLEDGMENTS

I would like to express my gratitude to the many people who saw me through this book; to all those who provided support, talked things over, read, wrote, offered comments, allowed me to quote their remarks and assisted in the editing and proofreading.

I want to thank my husband and my two boys, who supported and encouraged me in spite of all the time it took me away from them.

I would like to thank Primoz Bozic for keeping me accountable during the writing process. Beautiful Ulla Gaudin, Clarissa Grace, and Gladys Ato for always being there for me. Renae Christine for introducing me to the world of mentors and online communities; before I met you, I felt like such an odd duckling. Selena Soo, Richie Norton, Ben Hardy, and JLD for being the most incredible and supportive mentors - you helped me more than you'll ever know.

Last but not least, I want to thank the entire SPS crew and community - you are amazing, and I couldn't have done this without you.

INTRODUCTION

"Eevi gave me TONS of useful information that had never been covered or even mentioned in any of my reading, podcast listening and webinar attending! The information she provided will be invaluable as I get ready to launch my first children's book."
~ P. Costello, Ph.D., Author of Catalina And The King's Wall

When my first book was published some years ago, I felt lost and overwhelmed throughout the entire writing and marketing process. After months and months of frustrating research, I painstakingly put all the pieces together, but still felt like something was missing.

Most of the information out there was relevant only to writing and marketing books for adults – there seemed to be nothing specifically for children's authors. I so wished I could have had some guidance and support back then.

Many books later, I'm now in a position to share all that I've learned over the past couple of years. It's my hope that with this book, I'll be able to take months (if not years) off your learning curve so that you can enjoy the fun parts of creating your children's book.

I want to provide you with the most relevant and sought-after information, all easily accessible, in one single place. I've drawn on my experience working with many aspiring authors to create content that will help you during the process of writing your very own children's book. This includes:

- How to create and publish your book using my step-by-step blueprint – the exact process I use to create and publish my own books.
- A hand-selected list of highly qualified editors, illustrators, book formatters, and marketing strategists you can hire, without it costing you a fortune.
- Ways to find wonderful story ideas for your children's book.
- Industry standards for page and word count, based on the age group you are writing for.
- The key to writing book titles and descriptions that will grab customers' attention and make your book stand out.
- The exact tools you need (most of them free) to make your artwork and book look absolutely great.
- Templates of emails I use to hire editors and illustrators, plus the exact emails I send to ask influencers for reviews I can feature on my cover.

Throughout the book I feature various editors, illustrators, marketing specialists, and other services and service providers. Please note that I am not an affiliate. I'm not being compensated by any of these artists or service providers in any way. It's just my way of showing my appreciation for such an amazing community, and spreading the word about and among truly amazing people.

WHO AM I?

Who am I, you might ask, to be qualified to write this book? How can I help you? And most importantly, why should you listen to me?

Hi, I'm Yvonne. But as you may have already noticed, I go by Eevi. I have written and illustrated more than a dozen children's books, ranging from baby books to middle-grade chapter books, half of which have made it onto Amazon's bestseller lists. I'm fortunate enough to be able to make a living doing what I love most. I truly adore what I do, and with this book I'm trying to give back to the wonderful author community, so children can benefit from its wealth of creativity – because the greatest gift we can give our children is a passion for reading.

This book will save you hundreds of hours of research, not to mention financial resources.

While other aspiring children's book authors are experiencing years of frustration, you'll be able to experience the excitement and joy of sharing your books with loved ones, friends and fans around the world.

If you follow the steps outlined in this book, you'll soon be joining the ranks of published authors.

You may be wondering if you could figure out all this information on your own. And the answer is, probably. But there's surprisingly little help out there for self-published children's book authors when it comes to the actual building process, like formatting and marketing.

Having put in hours and hours of work, made a lot of time-consuming and expensive mistakes, wasted quite a lot of money on illustrators, software, and other unnecessary things, I'm in the perfect position to provide you with the help and support you need to achieve your dream of writing your very own children's book.

In the past, we had gatekeepers like agents and publishers. You would write your book, send it off to a publisher and wait for months, only to be rejected. Then you had to repeat the process again. And again. But that's no longer the case. If you're motivated and willing to put in the work, you can write a book and publish it. And you'll be rewarded for it, many times over and beyond any monetary measures.

The publishing landscape is changing.

The indie author market has been thriving and growing for quite some time now. And as self-published authors become more professional and polished, an increasing number of readers dip into this relatively new market. Browse through Amazon's book offerings, and most of the time you won't be able to distinguish between self-published and traditionally published books, especially with the increasing popularity of ebooks.

Regardless of which book format you prefer, *How To Self-Publish A Children's Book* will guide you through the creation of both the paperback and ebook version of your children's book.

I have interviewed and surveyed close to a hundred aspiring children's book authors to make this guide as relevant and actionable as possible, addressing all the pain points felt by someone that is trying to write and publish a successful children's book.

From finding an idea, all the way through to uploading your finished manuscript and illustrations, this book will guide and support you throughout this exciting process.

It includes a number of swipe files, templates, and resources to help you with the process and creation of your children's book. I have also included a number of service providers, such as illustrators, editors, and book formatters, each hand-selected to get you off to a good start.

To help you find these resources easily, I have indicated them with an arrow ↘ throughout the book. You can view and download each file at http://www.eevijones.com/book-downloads. It's easiest to just bookmark this page so you can refer to it as quickly and easily as possible.

I truly hope you find that this book provides you with everything you need to make your dream of writing a children's book a reality. I can't wait to see you succeed. Once you hit the publish button, I would love to hear from you and learn about your book. You can contact me at hello@eevijones.com. I read every message I receive.

You've taken the first step. You're holding this book in your hands. Your desire has moved up to the next level. You've taken the initiative to fulfill your dream. And I am so excited for you!

Always remember, the number one thing that will set you apart is taking action.

So let's get started.

With my deepest gratitude,

~ E.

Part I
THE CREATIVE PROCESS

CHAPTER ONE

PREPARATION AND SETTING EXPECTATIONS

I n order to stay on top of the many tasks involved in writing, illustrating, and publishing your children's book, we will need a process; a specific order in which to do things, because there's just so much to do when creating a children's book.

In this section we're going to focus on the creative process. One of my favorite explanations of the creative process comes from Kazu Kibuishi, a Japanese-American graphic novel author and illustrator. He once tweeted:

This tweet describes an emotional rollercoaster. Throughout the book-writing process, we experience all of these thoughts and emotions. I want you to know this is completely normal. We all get discouraged at times. The trick is to stick with it! To persevere. To keep on pushing through the process. Because at the very end, you'll be holding your very own children's book in your hands!

THIS BOOK IS FOR YOU IF YOU WANT TO LEARN HOW TO:

- **WRITE** your very own book for children aged 2–12
- **FIND** and develop an enticing story idea
- **CHOOSE THE BEST SETUP** for different age groups
- **CREATE** a storyboard
- **WRITE** an enticing blurb to go on the back cover of your book
- **FIND & HIRE** an illustrator/ editor/ cover designer/ internal designer
- **MAKE** use of mostly free online resources
- **UPLOAD & PUBLISH** your finished paperback and ebook
- **PROMOTE** your completed book

THIS BOOK IS NOT FOR YOU IF:

- You want to write young adult fiction (YA). If you're looking to write books for ages 12 and beyond, check out Chandler Bolt's Self-Publishing School (http://bit.ly/Self-PublishingSchool), where he teaches you to do just that.
- You've already written multiple successful children's books.
- You are not willing to put some work into this amazing dream of yours.

DISCLAIMER

- This book covers children's books and chapter books with illustrations for children aged 2–12. It does not cover young adult fiction or the creation of animated ebooks.
- While I have aimed to lay out the most cost-effective ways possible, the ultimate costs of your book depend entirely on your preferences and the decisions you make throughout the book-creation process.
- My formatting and submission advice relies on Createspace's and KDP's dimensions and guidelines, simply because that's what I've been using and because they are the most popular and most cost-effective choices at the time of writing.
- Currently, Createspace does NOT offer a hardcover choice for any of its books. If you wish to go with a hardcover, try places such as **Ingramspark**, **Lightning-Press**, or **Lulu**.

SELF-PUBLISHING VS. TRADITIONAL PUBLISHING

Before we get too far into the actual book writing, I want to take a minute to talk about your publishing options as an author (yes, you are going to be an author soon and should get used to calling yourself one). Authors now have a choice as to how they publish their books. The first question I'm usually asked when people learn I'm a children's book author is, have my books been published via the traditional route, or have I self-published them?

I always answer the same way: While I did jump through all the hoops of query-writing and manuscript-sending, which resulted in the offer of a publishing deal, I ended up turning it down and instead decided to publish my book on my own, under what was to become my own imprint.

I weighed my options carefully. And while it was a number of years ago, the reasons for my decision still hold true today. Yes – receiving that coveted book deal seems glamorous; prestigious, even. It's the ultimate dream of every author. But it's important to consider the advantages and disadvantages of each option.

You may, of course have your own reasons for choosing one way over the other, but here is the list of factors that led to my decision to go the self-publishing route.

1. One of the most often-cited advantages of traditional publishing is the fact that the publisher is able to distribute your book through bookstores and the like. But even if your book does make its way into your neighborhood Barnes and Noble, it will soon be pulled off the shelves again to make room for the next round of newly published reads.

2. Another perceived advantage of being traditionally published is that the publisher will help the author with marketing. As most authors aren't familiar with this side of publishing, in the past it was an important factor in the decision-making process. Nowadays, however, unless you are already a well-established author with a major following, publishing houses no longer pour money into a marketing plan or strategy for your book – they expect the author to do all that on their own.

3. Maintaining control over multiple different publishing aspects is also an important factor to consider. For example, when you decide to self-publish, you are the one setting the price the book will sell for. You are the one who gets to choose the illustrator. And you are the one who sets the publication date. Yes, you are also the one who will have to bear all the costs involved in creating your book, but you will be the one reaping the majority of the benefits.

4. Royalties. Yes, the publishing platform you choose will take a percentage of your book's revenue, but that percentage is nothing compared to what a traditional publishing house would pocket.

In fact, royalties were such an important factor during my decision-making process that I'd like to expound on this a bit further.

Because of the underlying economic structure of children's books, the earnings of a children's book author are much lower than those of an adult author. In traditional publishing, write for young people, and you are worth half as much as a peer writing for adults.

Not so with self-publishing.

When it comes to ebooks, children's books can make as much, if not more in royalties for the self-published author.

And while a traditionally published children's book author brings in royalties between 10 - 12.5% for a paperback, a self-published author can make around 27% per sold book, depending on things such as the price you set for your book, page count, trim size, and the like. That's more than double! (This approximate percentage is based on a sales price that is competitive with similar books.)

And in the children's book market, print is strong. According to a recent Nielsen study, the children's/YA market represents roughly 35% of the overall print market (slightly smaller than the adult nonfiction market, but slightly bigger than the adult fiction market).

Here's Createspace's handy-dandy tool to calculate your royalties per manufactured book. Feel free to play around with the number of pages, list price, and other interior settings to see possible earnings.

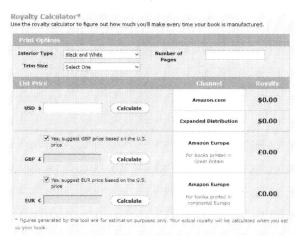

[https://www.createspace.com/Products/Book]

If I were given the chance to publish with a traditional publisher, would I take it, knowing what I know now? For the right terms and conditions, absolutely. But for now, I won't spend any more time or energy chasing a deal. Instead, I'll focus on what I love most: writing and illustrating children's books, and teachings others to do the same.

Self-published authors now win awards, sign movie deals, and make the New York Times bestseller list. And there are plenty of self-published authors that take home bigger and fatter royalty checks than many traditionally published authors.

Nowadays, it's no longer about *how* you've been published, but that you took your destiny into your own hands, and had the balls, passion, and perseverance to simply do so. It's about *what* you've created, and *whom* you've created it for.

The medium only becomes relevant if it becomes something that you let yourself be defined by.

How To Self-Publish A Children's Book is for those who want to publish a book themselves. However, if you are set on publishing the traditional way, here are two books I'd recommend:

- *Closing The Deal On Your Terms*, by Kristine Kathryn Rusch
- *How Authors Sell Publishing Rights*, by Helen Sedwick & Orna Ross

MINDSET IS EVERYTHING

One of the most important steps in writing a book is to create a plan. It is also the most overlooked step. According to a New York Times article by Joseph Epstein, about 81 percent of Americans want to write a book. But only around 1-3 percent actually end up doing so? Why is that?

Writing a book is far from easy. It requires dedication, time, and most importantly, passion. But with a little bit of planning, we can beat those odds of being one of those that never start (or never finish) their book.

YOUR MINDSET

Let's start with your mindset. Ask yourself: why do you want to write this children's book in the first place? If we can answer this question, we will always have a reason to come back to if we feel too tired, or think we don't have the time to work on our book. Here are some of the reasons my clients have given:

- *"I always had this story in my head and want to finally put it on paper."*
- *"My mom used to always tell me this story at bedtime when I was little, and I want to preserve these treasured memories."*
- *"I want to see the joy in my daughter's face when I read it to her."*
- *"I want to pass on my experiences to others in the form of a children's book."*
- *"I want to educate and teach in an area that I believe is currently not sufficiently covered."*
- *"I would like to follow my passion of becoming a children's book author."*

Do any of these *WHY*s resonate with you? What are your *WHY*s? Download your ➘ *Why Sheet* and write down your reasons, and hang them next to your desk, where you can easily see them whenever you look up from your computer. Use them to remind yourself why you're putting all this hard work into writing your children's book.

TACKLING OVERWHELM

Overwhelm is often an enormous contributor to giving up on your dream. To prevent this, we'll take things one small and manageable step at a time. How do we eat an elephant? Bite by bite.

One of the techniques I'd like to introduce here is jotting down the individual steps for making your children's book, and then scheduling them in your calendar. We all know that if something isn't scheduled, it's far less likely to happen.

You can schedule the steps in a way that works best for you, but do schedule them, as this will greatly influence whether or not you'll finish this amazing project of yours.

Let's look at some of the project milestones you might identify for your work. Illustrations, for example, are of course only relevant if you wish to include them in your book. You could dedicate a week to each milestone, or a whole month. The timeframe doesn't matter, as long as you actually create a timeline and roadmap to guide you through the process. For now, don't worry about what each of these milestones entails. We'll go into more detail later on in this book.

To help you get started, I have created the visual ◥ *Roadmap* below. Simply download the pdf and schedule the individual milestones in your calendar.

◥ [http://www.eevijones.com/book-downloads]

YOUR TO DOs FOR THIS CHAPTER:

☐ Write down your WHYs on your *Why Sheet* and hang them next to your computer
☐ Download your *Roadmap*
☐ Schedule the above outlined milestones in your calendar

Be sure to use all the lists, templates, and swipe files I've provided you with. You can find them here:

↘ http://www.eevijones.com/book-downloads

CHAPTER TWO

GETTING STARTED

I want to be completely up front with you – writing your own children's book can be pricey. But it doesn't have to be. There are certain aspects you shouldn't skimp on, like hiring a professional editor and cover designer. However, things like illustrating your book yourself, or choosing paperback over hardcover, will save you money.

COSTS INVOLVED IN CREATING YOUR CHILDREN'S BOOK

The "specs" – length, trim size, number of pages, color vs. black and white, and type of cover, will all affect the price set by the printing platform.

In the simplest terms, anything you charge in addition to this base price will be your markup, the money you'll use to cover the expenses you incurred during the making of your book.

PRICING YOUR BOOK

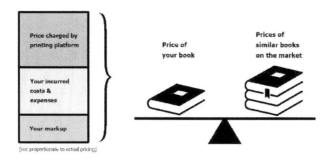

Ask yourself the following questions:

1. How important are professional illustrations to me?

2. How much am I willing to pay for a professional editor?

3. How much can I do on my own?

4. Is it more important to me to make the price as attractive as possible (low or compatible pricing) or as profitable as possible (high pricing)?

If I could invest in only two things throughout this entire process, I would choose an experienced editor (if your manuscript is more than 600 words) and a professional cover designer!

―――――――――◆◆◆◆◆――――――――

FIND AN AMAZING IDEA FOR YOUR CHILDREN'S BOOK

You're reading this book, so it's very likely that you already have an idea for your book in mind. Maybe an entire story has been developing within you for the longest time. Maybe you thought of a character during those long nights you were trying to get your child to sleep. Or maybe you remember stories from your childhood; stories that you now wish to breathe new life into. If that's the case, congratulations! You can skip this part and move on to the next.

If you don't yet have a story in mind, there are a number of ways we can get your creative juices flowing. It's important to keep in mind the age group you'd like to write for, as this will greatly influence the use of illustrations and the amount and type of text you'll write.

But for now, let's focus on finding the right story for you to write. Below are some of the ways I've found topics for my own children's books.

HOW TO DISCOVER IDEAS WITHIN YOU

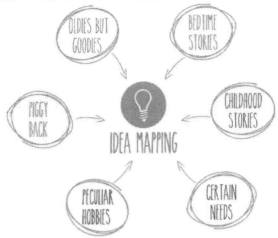

1. BEDTIME STORIES: Do you make up bedtime stories for your children? These stories often feature the most beloved of all characters, and are treasured by both you and your child. For example, in the Winnie-the-Pooh stories, A.A. Milne brought to life his son Christopher Robin's toys, including a chubby bear, a donkey, a tiger, a kangaroo, and a piglet.

2. CHILDHOOD STORIES: The way things used to be … With the rise of technology, things change at a much quicker pace. Are your little ones curious about your childhood? I know mine were. They kept asking me what it was like growing up in former East Germany, so one day I decided to write down my most precious childhood memories in a book. It was so popular among my family and friends that I published it, and *Growing Up In East Germany* was born.

3. CERTAIN NEEDS: Did something happen that prompted you to make up a story? Back when my two-year-old was having difficulties transitioning from his potty chair to the toilet (he was already potty trained), I looked for a book that would help him. As there were none that addressed this particular problem, I decided to write and illustrate my own, and *Teeny Totty Uses Mama's Big Potty* was born.

4. PECULIAR HOBBIES: Does your child have a hobby, interest, or passion that you can't find a book about? Use this as an opportunity and write your own! Chances are there are many other kids out there obsessed with the exact same thing. My youngest was absolutely crazy about lawn mowers, for example. I didn't like the selection I saw on Amazon, so I wrote *The Little Mower That Could.*

5. PIGGYBACK: Ask yourself, what animals/ topics/ toys are really big right now? Of course you can't just copy characters directly, due to copyright rules, but you can create similar ones. Let's say Disney just released a new movie about dinosaurs. Chances are you'll see a lot of little die-hard dinosaur fans walking around right after the first screening. You can piggyback on that opportunity and create your very own dinosaur story. In fact, that's what I did after the movie Monster Trucks was released in 2016 – I wrote and illustrated *Lil Foot The Monster Truck.*

6. OLDIES BUT GOODIES: If a theme has proven itself over and over again, why not revamp and reuse it? People do this all the time, for example in mysteries and thrillers. You could do the same for children's books. How about a mighty little girl, like Pippi Longstocking? Or a kind machine, like Thomas the Tank Engine? The possibilities are truly endless.

As you can see, I took some of these opportunities that presented themselves and grabbed them by the horns. I had a ton of fun writing these stories, and my little ones were over the moon reading the books with me (over and over again).

I have prepared an ⬎ *Idea Sheet* you can use to jot down the ideas you come up with during your brainstorming sessions. Write down anything that comes to mind – even if you think it's really silly, write it down. You can always cross them off later.

Once you have filled out your *Idea Sheet*, you should have a great list of brainstormed ideas that you can use to develop your story.

To help you with your brainstorming session, I've also compiled a list of ⬎ *300 Things Children Like*.

Consider the people who are actually buying your books – parents! Think about what would help them. What do they want their kids to learn? What fits with their worldview? What would they tell other parents about or leave a good review for?

──────────◆◦◆◦◆──────────

KNOW YOUR AUDIENCE

Children's books come from inspiration. But inspiration is only part of the story.

Aspiring children's book authors often forget that they're essentially creating a book that a parent is going to buy; so make sure you have a particular audience in mind. Not all books are for everyone, but the more relatable the book, the more popular.

The main buyer age of children's books is between 30 and 44. Females make up more than 70% of these buyers. (They are also more likely to discuss and recommend a book they and their kids enjoyed. In fact, buyers of children's books are more easily influenced by the recommendation of family and friends than any other book category.)

When drafting your story, ask yourself questions like these:

1. Who will buy your book?
2. Who will read your book? (child or parent)

3. Will your book appeal to girls or boys or both?
4. What type of household do they live in?
5. Where do they do their shopping?
6. What classrooms would use your book and why?
7. What grade is your book appropriate for?
8. What lessons would parents/ teachers want to draw from your book?

The best way to identify your audience is to research them. Even if you already have a particular audience in mind, spend some time learning more, because the more you know, the more relatable your book will be.

You could spend time within age groups you're targeting, or talk to parents and teachers. Remember that your book will have to please parents and teachers just as much as children.

You could search for age group trends and consumer trends in general via sites like *Slideshare* (https://www.slideshare.net), or frequent the *US Census* (https://www.census.gov) that provides detailed demographic data.

And sites like *Nielsen.com* provide data to find out how particular demographic clusters behave.

Or you could conduct a survey within your social media channels via *Surveymonkey.com* and ask your friends & family.

With the right planning and understanding of your marketplace and your audience, you can place yourself several steps ahead of everyone else and build a path to success.

◆◆●◆●◆

THE STRUCTURE OF YOUR CHILDREN'S BOOK

In this section we'll look at how many pages your book should have, the number of illustrations to include, and the general layout and structure. The way you set up your book will greatly depend on the type of children's book and the age group you are targeting. This is why in the previous section we began with finding an idea to write about (see your *Idea Sheet*).

There are a number of different types of children's books, and below is a list of the most common ones. Please be aware that there is no one true or accurate list of children's book categories. This is simply meant to give you an idea of the basic word count and the associated age group.

	CATEGORY	AGE	WORDS	PG	EXAMPLE	# OF ILLUSTR.
1	Picture book	0–3	0	32	*Good Night, Gorilla*	Every page
2	Young picture book	2–5	200–400	32	*Jamberry*	Every page
3	Trade picture Book	4–8	400–800	32	*Knuffle Bunny*	Every page
4	Picture story book	6–10	1,000–3,000	32	*Ocean Commotion*	Every page
5	Chapter book	6–10	3,000–10,000	50	*Amelia Bedelia*	Almost every page (b&w)
6	Middle-grade book	8–12	15,000–40,000	82	*The Magic Tree House*	12+ illustr. (b&w)

Picture books for ages 0–3 tend to focus on basic concepts such as color, shapes, sounds, and so on. These types of books are often referred to as "concept books," because they convey concepts or simple information rather than complex stories.

Young picture books for ages 2–5 are picture books that cater to very young children. They are often counting books, novelty books, or bedtime books. They are often written in rhyme, using between 200 and 400 words. This type of book can be quite challenging to write, because the use of very simple vocabulary can be limiting. This is one of my favorite categories.

Trade picture books for ages 4–8 are the standard picture books you see in bookstores. With a word count of 400–800, these books are perfect for kids who are ready to explore the world. The stories often address issues they will face in their everyday lives.

Picture story books for ages 6–10 are trade picture books catering to older kids. In most cases there are images on every page, and the word count is now between 1,000 and 3,000.

Chapter books for ages 6–10 are transitionary books, broken down into short simple chapters to prepare children for reading novels. With a word count of 3,000–10,000, these books contain only a few illustrations and tend to be written in series that repeat a simple plot format. They are almost never written in rhyme. (See below for more on the structure of chapter books.)

Middle-grade books are written for kids approximately 8–12 years old. As with all children's books, the language should complement their vocabulary level. Middle-grade stories tend to have strong themes with plenty of adventure. Parents are generally absent, happy endings are the norm, and the protagonist is always in the age range of the reader, or slightly older.

As you can see, the various types of children's books differ greatly in both their use of images and the number of words. This makes your decision on what age group you are planning to write for very important, as every subsequent decision will depend on what type of book you're choosing to write.

It's generally a great idea to find a book (or a number of books) similar to what you have in mind, and use the word count, number of pages, and number of illustrations as a guide for your own book.

The website https://www.renaissance.com (for teachers) is a great resource for researching the word count of published books.

I have created a ⬎ *Structure Sheet* that you can use to fill in information about similar books, including their category, targeted age group, word count, number of pages, and number of illustrations. I urge you to do this research and to fill out this *Structure Sheet*, as we'll refer to it in subsequent chapters.

AN EXTRA WORD ON CHAPTER BOOKS

I love chapter books. They provide such a wonderful transition, from beginning to intermediate readers. The stories are told primarily through prose, rather than pictures, but still contain plenty of illustrations.

As we have learned, chapter books are usually for children aged 6–10, and have a word count of 3,000–10,000. As the name implies, they are divided into chapters, usually 10–12 of them, each about 350–800 words long. The chapters often have a fun or intriguing title, and end with a cliffhanger to keep the reader turning those pages.

I've created a ⬎ *Chapter Book Template* to help you divide your story into separate sections. I use it for all the chapter books in my *"Amulet of Amser"* series.

ORIENTATION

When it comes to picture books, there are a number of different orientations to choose from. (These don't apply to chapter books or books for older children, as those usually feature the 5½" x 8" format.)

There is no set rule, however. Rather, it's an oversimplified observation. I personally prefer the square format for my picture books.

VERTICAL	**HORIZONTAL**	**SQUARE**
(good to use with character-based books)	(to illustrate a journey-like story)	(instructional books)
Cat In The Hat	Maisy Books	Berenstain Bears
5-Minute Story Books	Knuffle Bunny	Clifford
Fairy Tales	The Magic School Bus	Potty-Training Books

When you've laid the foundation for your book by filling out the *Structure Sheet*, you'll be ready to start with the actual writing process. You finally get to put to paper what you've been wanting to share with the world for so very long.

YOUR TO DOs FOR THIS CHAPTER:

☐ Find an amazing idea for your book with the *Idea Sheet*
☐ If you need further inspiration, download my *300 Things Children Like* list
☐ Decide on the age group and structure of your children's book, and find books that are similar to what you have in mind and note them on the *Structure Sheet*
☐ If you're writing a chapter book, use my *Chapter Book Formula* to help you divide your story into separate sections

Be sure to use all the lists, templates, and swipe files I've provided you with. You can find them here:

↘ http://www.eevijones.com/book-downloads

CHAPTER THREE

WRITING YOUR STORY

In this chapter, we'll first look at some of the tools we can use to make writing a super fun experience. We'll examine some of the main elements successful children's book authors use in their stories, and will look at different writing styles. We'll create storyboards to develop an idea and the layout of your images, and will think about how to come up with the perfect title – one of the most important aspects of your book.

By the end of this chapter, you will also know how to write the following:

- BLURB – the text that goes on the back cover of your book
- ABOUT THE AUTHOR – a short, fun author bio
- CALL TO ACTION – the section that asks the reader either for their email address, or for a review (or both)
- OTHER WORKS BY THIS AUTHOR – the section that tells the reader about your other books

HELPFUL TOOLS

There are a number of tools we can use to make the planning and writing process easier – and, more importantly, more fun. Most (not all) of these are free, so check them out and see which might work for you.

- **Scrivener**   word-processing program & outline designed for authors (**http://www.literatureandlatte.com/scrivener.php**)
- **Thesaurus**   a comprehensive search engine for synonyms (**http://www.thesaurus.com**)
- **Google Docs**   cloud-based tool, easy to share with illustrators (**https://docs.google.com**)
- **Evernote**   cloud-based; apps for phone, ideas file, images file, easy to share and edit (**https://evernote.com**)
- **Rhyme Zone**   a comprehensive search engine for rhymes (**http://rhymezone.com**)
- **OneLook**   a dictionary on steroids; its reverse dictionary feature lets you describe a concept and receive a list of words and phrases related to that concept (**http://www.onelook.com**)
- **WrittenSound**   A dictionary of onomatopoeia (sound words) and words of imitative origin (**http://www.writtensound.com/index.php**)
- **PlainLanguage**   simplify your words and phrases (**http://www.plainlanguage.gov/howto/wordsuggestions/simplewords.cfm**)
- **Story Openings**   An extensive list of story openings (**http://www.folktale.net/openers.html**)
- **Story Endings**   An extensive list of story endings (**http://www.folktale.net/endings.html**)
- **Mind Mapping**
  - **Xmind**   free & paid version (**http://www.xmind.net**)
  - **Mindjet**   free trial (**https://www.mindjet.com**)

•**Freemind**	free
	(**https://freemind.en.softonic.com**)
•**Mindmeister**	free & paid version
	(**https://www.mindmeister.com**)

I've included a more extensive list of great resources toward the end of the book. Please note that I am not an affiliate to any of these sites or programs – I'm just passing on what I know has brought great value to many authors' writing processes.

You don't have to use any of these resources listed above – use what works best for you. For example, I use a simple Excel sheet to outline my story, and then migrate to Microsoft Word for the actual writing of the book.

◆◆●◆◆

FIVE STORY ELEMENTS

Now that you have an exciting story idea in mind and a number of helpful tools to work with, we can begin to write your story.

Your unique and inspired story idea is only as strong as the way in which you tell it. Be sure to be clear about your core message. Always ask yourself what you want your core message to be.

In children's books, characters reign supreme.

The plot is simply a series of obstacles that get in the way of a single objective. And much about setting, plot, and character depend on the age group. In general, kids want to relate to kids that are just a bit older than them.

Good stories are carefully designed. And they tend to be simple. It's about composition. There's a beginning, a middle, and an end; there are actions, scenes, and emotions. The elements aren't always the same, but these are the five that top authors often use:

1. **Unforgettable characters:** The best characters have strong personalities, make bold moves, and go after their dreams against all

odds. Children fall in love with them and want to be like them. Children always want to be able to relate to the character in some way. Almost every person has felt like an outsider or has had their morals questioned. Characters who remind kids of themselves are the most memorable.

2. Suspenseful action/hook: Many authors shy away from beginning their story with an action, such as a shocking or unexpected event, but this is a very effective way to draw in young readers. Other ways to hook the reader at the start include:

- description of a strange character
- an interesting or unusual setting
- surprising dialogue
- a problem

Consistent action throughout your story is key, as it will hold the reader's attention. Chapter books, for example, usually end each chapter with a cliffhanger, to ensure the reader keeps turning the pages.

3. Realistic dialogue: Children like to read stories that sound like they talk. Listen to conversations you hear around you; none of them will sound like the nicely flowing, full sentences you learned to write in school. Make sure you're using age-appropriate language that kids will understand, connect with, and relate to. If you are unsure about the language level of your target audience, be sure to spend some time among kids of that particular age. Go to libraries, visit friends with kids, or simply read children's books to get a feel for the language used.

4. Story line: Be sure to provide obstacles and challenges for your characters; some sort of escalation. Also note that little ones like happy endings and a solution to a problem. If your story lacks a happy ending, you risk upsetting the reader, or at least leaving them dissatisfied.

5. The instant recall factor: You want your book's character to remain in the minds of your little readers long after they've read your book. If kids ask to read it over and over again, you can consider your story a success.

Kids crave memorable stories and captivating characters that empower them. You can achieve this first and foremost by writing an amazing story; then you can include great illustrations, perhaps rhyme. The sky's your limit.

> HOOK → PLACE → PROBLEM → INCIDENT →
> ESCALATION → RESOLUTION → RECALL

While the sequence and rhythm of events is very important, please keep in mind that not all stories have the same structure. There is no one formula, because following a formula would rob stories of their true potential. Yes, it's important to have an intentional structure, but if it doesn't fit, don't force it.

Children value creativity and individuality. There is no one way to draw. No one way to paint. No one way to write. It's about being uniquely you, lending your unique voice to your unique story. That's why you shouldn't be afraid of the way YOU write and YOU draw, because that's what sets you apart. Diversity is important. Tell YOUR story.

CHOOSING A WRITING STYLE (AND STICKING WITH IT)

Your writing style will depend greatly on the age group you are writing for, the associated word count, the story you're telling, and, of course, your own preferences. Here are some styles worth considering:

- **RHYME:** If you decide to write your book in rhyme, you need to make the rhyme very, very good. Make sure lines have the same syllable counts and rhythms. Don't force bad rhymes or skip rhyming. Be persistent. And consistent.

- **PAST OR PRESENT TENSE:** Kids like books in the present tense, as it actively engages them in the story. They're experiencing it as it happens, rather than being removed from something that happened in the past. If, however, you're telling a story that is specific to a certain event or time, you might want to tell it in past tense, because it's a finite event that took place once upon a time.

- **FIRST OR THIRD PERSON:** Whose point of view the story is told from is one of the most important decisions an author has to make. Is the main character the central focus on every page, with everything happening to them? Is it helpful to see the events that are happening through their eyes? If yes, then first person might be a good choice. If not, a third person narrator's voice may give you more freedom and flexibility.

There is no right or wrong approach; it's simply a question of style. Once you have chosen your style, however, you will need to stick to it throughout the book.

TIPS FOR YOUR WRITING PROCESS

- Keep a notepad or recording device handy at all times to capture your ideas. You never know when the perfect wording might jump into your head. You want to write it down right away so it doesn't slip your mind again. If, for example, some of your best ideas come to you at night, keep a notepad and pen next to your bed.

- Block off specific writing times. What gets scheduled gets done. Believe me, if you don't, you won't find time. Make writing a priority and plan your sessions, even if it's just 30 minutes a day.

- Set yourself a daily writing goal. It may only be a few words a day, but that's better than none. You'll always have your *WHY-Sheet* to fall back on, reminding you *why* you wanted to write this beautiful book to begin with.

- Remember the age of the children you're writing for. Keep the number of words from the table in Chapter 2 in mind, and use vocabulary suited to your target audience. Ask yourself whether the book is meant to be read by parents or by early readers.

TESTING YOUR STORY

If you want to go the extra mile and ensure your book is as good as it can possibly be, go and test your book on kids your target age. Maybe you can go and ask a local library if they'd let you read your book during their weekly story time. Or maybe your son or daughter's teacher will allow you to come by and read your book to the class. The more you can test your story, the better.

What are the kids' reaction? Are they engaged? Are they asking follow up question? Were there some words they didn't understand?

Paying attention to their attentiveness and reaction can be a great indicator how well your book will be perceived once published. And if some words needed further clarification, you know not to use this particular term and instead use a more age appropriate word. This is your target audience, so doing some direct 'market research' can only be of benefit to you. Plus, you're getting the word out there already about your upcoming book. Creating buzz prior to the actual book release is always a big plus and part of a great marketing strategy.

Below is the 'market research' I conducted as I wrote my book *Growing Up In East Germany*. Having read the book before its actual publishing was truly insightful and invaluable as it let me know where the book needed tweaking. Plus, it was a lot of fun, for both me and the 1st graders.

GIVING YOUR BOOK A TITLE

Once your book is completed, and before you send anything to an illustrator and cover designer, it's time to think about a winning title for your book!

I'm quite certain you already have a title for your book in mind. In fact, it's probably something you've been thinking long and hard about for some time.

Yes, we want a clever, funny title that lets your story's personality shine through. But something we want just as much (if not more) is for readers to actually find your book! And this will be very hard to do if you don't name it properly.

Now don't get me wrong. There is no one proper way of naming a book, but there is a right approach and a wrong approach. Unless buyers already know about you, your book, and its title, most will search for a book using keywords. So in order for your book to be found more easily, we will need to include the most descriptive and most fitting keyword(s) in your book's title.

To illustrate, I have included some of my own book titles as examples.

KEYWORD	TITLE
Garbage trucks	*The **Garbage Trucks** Are Here*
(Lawn) mowers	*The Little **Mower** That Could*
Monster trucks	*Lil Foot The **Monster Truck***

I could have named my garbage truck book something more creative, like *What Rumbles Through The Streets?* But this title alone wouldn't tell people what the book was about. And without the keyword in the title, it would make searching for it a lot harder as well. On the other hand, the title *The Garbage Trucks Are Here* will show up if potential buyers enter "garbage truck" in Amazon's search bar.

Remember that we can give the book a subtitle, so we can include a synonym of our keyword here as well. The title and subtitle of this book are a great example:

KEYWORDS	Children's Book, Writing, Illustrating, Publishing
TITLE	How To Self-**Publish** A **Children's Book**
SUBTITLE	Everything You Need To Know To **Write, Illustrate, Publish**, And Market Your Paperback And Ebook

While we want to pay attention to including the right terms in our title, we also need to make sure we don't include any awkward wording, something that a potential reader would never use to search for a book like yours.

Numbers, unusual spelling, or unnecessary punctuation marks such as a hyphen, colon, or brackets should be avoided. I wish I'd known this before deciding on the title of my first book, as my title broke all kinds of rules, making it much harder to be found and discovered by a potential reader.

KEYWORDS	Military Families, Soldiers
TITLE	*Closing the Gap: Understanding Your Service(wo)man*

My keywords are nowhere to be found within my title. It also contains a colon and brackets. Honestly, would you ever think of entering "Service(wo)man" into Amazon's search bar when you're looking for a book about military families? Probably not. Lesson(s) learned!

TESTING YOUR TITLE

Want to know if you've got a killer title for your book? With Lulu.com's Title Scorer Test you can put your title to the scientific test and find out whether it has what it takes for bestseller success.

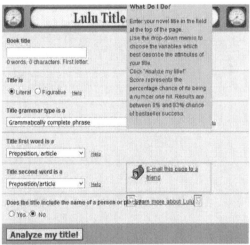

[http://www.lulu.com/titlescorer/index.php]

Or you can employ the old-fashioned way and simply ask your friends, family, social media channels and communities what they'd prefer. For example, create a poll within Facebook and let others vote on the title choices you provide them with. Your friends and family will love to help you with this.

To summarize, when creating your book's optimized title:

1. Use keywords that potential readers might use when looking for a book on your topic.
2. Make your title as clear and direct as possible.
3. Make use of a subtitle, including a synonym of your keyword.
4. Try to refrain from using numbers, unusual spelling, or unnecessary punctuation marks.

———————— ◆◆●◆◆ ————————

If you want your editor to go over your table of contents (for chapter books only), copyright page, about the author page, and so on, it's a good idea to create those at the same time as writing the book, so they can be included when you send everything off to your editor. (To see what to include in a copyright page, please go to chapter 7.)

———————— ◆◆●◆◆ ————————

BLURB / TEXT FOR BACK COVER

We've learned how important our book's title is in terms of discoverability and grabbing a potential buyer's attention. But the words we use on our book's back cover are often the reason a reader decides to buy (or not to buy) our book.

A book cover blurb is a short (around 200–250 words) description of your book. If written well, it can be one of the most important marketing tools, as it hooks the reader, convincing them to buy.

To get a feel for what makes a great blurb, be sure to look at some similar books to yours. Pay special attention to length, word choice, and the style they are written in. That's usually a great way to see what your audience expects and is used to.

Make the blurb easily readable either by using bullet points (for non-fiction), or by breaking it up into short paragraphs.

Try to think like a parent who's looking for a new book for her child. What would make her interested in your book?

And most importantly, try to include a number of keywords that apply to your story and theme. But do this in a natural, uncontrived way to maintain a natural flow.

If your book has received a glowing editorial review, you could include a short excerpt of this in your blurb. Or if you have received praise from a well-known individual or expert within the book's subject area, be sure to display that.

This is a partial screenshot of the back cover of my very first children's book, *Teeny Totty Uses Mama's Big Potty – Transition From Potty Chair To Toilet*. It includes both keywords and little snippets of experts' reviews.

Keywords

"Today is the PERFECT day to learn something new. Something that only BIG kids can do."

Moving our children from potty to toilet can be almost as difficult as getting them on the potty in the first place. With warmth and sensitivity, Yvonne Jones guides little boys and girls through the challenges and rewards of transitioning from a potty to a grown-up toilet. A helpful "Note to Parents" is included.

"An adorable book that builds confidence and sets the stage for a successful transition."
- Colleen Brunetti, M.Ed., C.H.C., Potty Time Specialist

"Throughout the book, there are constant reminders that trying something new is fun. And good. And brave. And how being a Big Kid feels awesome."
- Jamie Glowacki, Author of "Oh Crap Potty Training"

"Hip, Hop, Hooray! Teeny Totty is the BEST at showing how to use the BIG Potty!"
- Teri Crane, Author of "Potty Train Your Child in Just One Day"

Review by top influencers and specialists

ABOUT THE AUTHOR

The About The Author snippet or page is optional. I personally like to include a short paragraph or two about myself to remind the reader that an actual person wrote (and illustrated) the book. That's especially useful if I'm including a Call to Action, where I ask the reader to consider writing a review (see CALL TO ACTION below).

This little snippet, written in the third person, also gives me a chance to connect, and to let my personality shine through a bit. Some authors also like to include a photo of themselves.

I include this information in the paperback as well as ebook version, the only difference being that the URL is hyperlinked in the ebook.

ABOUT THE AUTHOR

Yvonne was born in former East Germany to a German mother and a Vietnamese father – two adamant readers and advocates of literature. Thus, she spent an inordinate amount of her youth nosing through books that she shouldn't have been reading, and watching movies that she shouldn't have been watching. It was a good childhood.

Always drawing inspiration from her own two children, she loves to write about unique interests and aspires to find fun and exciting ways to have kids discover and learn about the magnificent marvels this world has to offer.

She can be found online at **www.Yvonne-Jones.com**.

CALL TO ACTION

As well as the About The Author paragraph(s), I urge you to include a Call to Action. In this case, we want to ask the reader to leave a review. Reviews are so very important, yet most readers don't realize how much impact a positive review can have on an author's future sales. Adding this little sentence toward the end of your book is an earnest request, so consider including it.

Note: within the ebook version, I usually also include the direct and clickable link to Amazon, to make accessing it as easy as possible.

A WORD BY THE AUTHOR

If you enjoyed this book, it would be wonderful if you could take a short minute to leave a lovely review on Amazon, as your kind feedback is very appreciated and so very important. It gives me, the author, encouragement for bad days when I want to take up scorpion petting. Thank you so very much for your time!

OTHER WORKS BY THIS AUTHOR

This page only applies if you have written more than one book. This is a great opportunity to introduce your other works to your readers. If he or she liked this book, chances are that your other books might be of interest as well.

MORE WORKS BY THIS AUTHOR

The Case of the Mona Lisa – The Amulet of Amser Series (1)
The Case of the Starry Night – The Amulet of Amser Series (2)
The Case of Venus de Milo – The Amulet of Amser Series (3)
The Garbage Trucks Are Here
The Impatient Little Vacuum
The Little Mower That Could
The Monster Numbers Book
A Gemstone Adventure – Prince Gem of Ology's Royal Quest
Safety Goose: Children's Safety – One Rhyme at a Time ***
Growing Up in East Germany – My Childhood Series (1)
Teeny Totty Uses Mama's Big Potty: Transition from Potty Chair to Toilet

*** Visit **www.Yvonne-Jones.com** to receive a FREE eBook version of this book

---

You'll notice that in addition to listing my other books, I have also included a little gift, prompting the reader to visit my website and provide me with his or her email in order to download a free ebook. These are some advanced techniques that are meant to grow your email list. But for now, don't worry about this, especially if this is your very first children's book.

Like before, the ebook version includes a clickable link to easily access my website.

YOUR TO DOs FOR THIS CHAPTER:

- ☐ Choose a writing style you are going to use throughout your book
- ☐ Do some keyword research and incorporate the best ones into your book's title and subtitle
- ☐ Write the extra pages for your book so you can submit those to your editor as well (Blurb, About the Author, Call to Action, Other Works by this Author)

Be sure to use all the lists, templates, and swipe files I've provided you with. You can find them here:

↘ http://www.eevijones.com/book-downloads

CHAPTER FOUR

YOUR BOOK EDITOR

Editing is a valuable investment in your book, as a good editor can turn your story from *okay* into *amazing*! Sadly, many aspiring authors believe they don't need an editor. But I'm a firm believer that a good editor is instrumental in making your book a success, because poor spelling, grammar, and book structure will reflect badly on your book's sales and reviews.

Your book and its message might be great, but if too many errors slip through, your readers will notice and voice their opinion in a review like the one below, which ultimately will lower your overall rating. No matter how many 5-star reviews you may have, many people also look at the lower ratings in order to decide whether or not to buy a book.

★☆☆☆☆ **Ever heard of an editor???**
By ▨▨▨ on August 20, 2016
Format: Kindle Edition | Verified Purchase

OMG!!! Why (or how) in the world does this book have so many 5-star reviews???? I really tried to read this book but was distracted by all the grammatical and spelling mistakes. I can only assume that English isn't the author's first language (which is totally fine, as mine isn't either), but come on!!! If you are going to publish your own book, put some pride into it and make use of some editorial services. Authors like this give selfpublished/Indie authors a bad reputation! If this book has a positive message, I missed it as I was too distracted by all the mistakes. I do not recommend this book!

[Edit] [Delete]

If your book is more than 600–800 words long, you should send it off to a professional editor. Even if your book has fewer words than that, having a picture book edited is fairly inexpensive and brings so much value with it, so why wouldn't you? Yes, you can go over it yourself. And yes, you can let your significant other read through it as well, but a third unbiased, independent, and professional person will make your manuscript so much better.

An editor usually charges for his/her services in one of three ways:

1. Cost per word
2. Cost per work/ flat rate
3. Cost per hour

I much prefer when an editor charges by cost per word, because I know exactly how much I'm going to be charged, as I am in control of the manuscript's word count.

However, cost per work (or a flat rate) sometimes makes more sense for very short works, such as picture books, where charging per word wouldn't make much sense for the editor.

Most editors who charge by the hour will quote based on a sample, and then stick to that quote as a fee. Hourly rates can also make sense for longer works, because a badly written book can take twice as long to edit as a clean manuscript. This then also favors writers who take the time to get their manuscript in good shape before submitting.

EDITING TYPES

Depending on where you live, there are three main types of editing, each requiring a different level of editorial feedback. Prices often differ slightly between these three types as well. When it's time for you to connect with an editor, you must clarify what is and isn't included in their services.

EDITING TYPES
1. Content editing
2. Copy editing
3. Proofreading

CONTENT EDITING:

This is sometimes called substantive, developmental, or structural editing. It aims to ensure that the structure, content, language, style and presentation of your book are suitable for its intended purpose and readership.

COPY EDITING:

Copy editing addresses accuracy, clarity, and consistency in a document. It does not involve significant rewriting, providing a single authorial voice, or tailoring text to a specific audience – these belong to a substantive edit outlined above. Copy editing covers:

- grammar
- punctuation
- subject-verb agreement
- spelling
- capitalization
- repeated words
- syntax
- inconsistencies
- omission

PROOFREADING:

Proofreading involves checking that the document is ready to be published. It includes making sure that all elements of the document are included and in the proper order, all amendments have been inserted, a unifying set style has been followed, and all spelling or punctuation errors have been rectified.

Since there is usually a small amount of text (less than 1,000 words) in picture books for younger kids, you may only need a copy edit rather than a content edit, to make sure there are no spelling or punctuation errors. I personally go with a combination of copy editing and proofreading if my manuscript is more than 800 words. It doesn't cost a lot more, and it's absolutely worth it.

If you are still not sure which editing service you need, simply ask the editor and he/she will help you figure it out.

WHAT TO LOOK FOR IN AN EDITOR

There are several things to consider when choosing book editors:

EDITOR CRITERIA

1. **GENRE:** As children's books differ greatly from adult books, you will want to make sure that the prospective editor has experience in editing children's books. He/she needs to understand what vocabulary is appropriate and suitable for each age group.

2. **RATE:** Definitely take rates into consideration, but don't select an editor solely on price. The highest rates don't necessarily mean the best editor, and the lowest rates could be a complete waste of money.

3. **RECOMMENDATION:** I personally put a lot of stock into recommended services, as this will help me understand another author's experience and what it is like to work with that particular editor.

When contacting a prospective editor, you'll want to inquire about the following (if this information isn't already specified on their website):

1. No-obligation quote
2. Time required to edit the entire manuscript (if payment is per hour, ask for estimated required hours)
3. Number of read-throughs included
4. Payment process
5. Sample edit

If this is your first time working with this editor, be sure to ask for a sample edit to make certain that you like his/her editing style, depth, and feedback. For regular books, I usually request a sample edit of a piece I have written of around 800–1,000 words. Since most children's books are much shorter, you will want to adjust that word count accordingly. The sample edit should definitely be shorter than the actual edit you're planning to hire him/her for.

To help you get started with your search for an editor, I've provided an ➘ *Editor Template* on how to contact a prospective editor and request a sample edit.

Once you decide to work with an editor, it helps to provide him or her with two or three bullet points on what you think he or she should know about your book and your audience. You could include information on the following points:

- Your book's target audience (age group)
- Word count
- Specific lingo you are using that is relevant to your story or specific to your industry
- The most important point you want to bring across with this book
- The overall tone you're going for (if relevant)
- Spaceholders for illustrations throughout your manuscript (so the editor knows what scenes will be supported visually)

Remember that editors are busy, so keep it as concise and brief as possible. In order to prevent any delays, you may also want to contact him or her a couple of weeks in advance in order to secure an opening that would best suit you and your timeline. I often book my editor 4-6 weeks prior to my actual manuscript submission, as the waiting list can be quite long at times.

Once you've booked an opening, send your final manuscript. Try not to tinker with the manuscript after you've submitted it (at least until you have the edited version back), as this often leads to you wanting to make changes, which defeats the whole purpose of having a professional editor look over your work.

Most editors will provide you with the following, once they've completed reading through your manuscript:

1. Completed edit with tracked changes and comments in the margins
2. Clean edit – tracked changes have been hidden, so all you see is what it would look like if you accepted all your editor's changes (can be easier to read than the tracked changes version)

It's important to note that an editor will NOT format your book (unless that is one of your editor's offered services).

To get the most out of your editor, you should let him or her edit everything that will be included in your book. For example, when sending my editor my manuscript, I usually include the following:

PACKAGE FOR EDITOR
1. Completed manuscript
2. Blurb (text) you are planning to have printed on the back of your book cover
3. ABOUT THE AUTHOR paragraph(s)
4. OTHER WORKS BY THIS AUTHOR page
5. CALL TO ACTION / REVIEW REQUEST paragraph(s)

YOUR TO DOs FOR THIS CHAPTER:

☐ Decide whether or not to hire an editor (if yes, what editing service would you require?)
☐ Find and hire an editor with the *Editor Template*
☐ Prepare Editor Package

Be sure to use all the lists, templates, and swipe files I've provided you with. You can find them here:

↘ http://www.eevijones.com/book-downloads

FEATURED EDITORS

Below is a list of editors I have either previously worked with or have had recommended to me by other authors. I've presented them in alphabetical order, indicating what editing services they offer.

Please note that I am not an affiliate to any of these services. I'm not being compensated by any of these service providers in any way. It's just my way of showing my appreciation for such an amazing community and is meant to spread the word about and among truly amazing people.

BILLINGTON MEDIA (http:/www.billingtonmedia.com)
Sarah has worked with USA Today and Amazon bestselling authors and does content, copy, and line editing. She has experience with Young Adult, Middle Grade & Junior Fiction. Free quotes are provided.

KHELSEA PURVIS (https://khelseapurvis.com)
Khelsea offers proofreading services. Contact her for rates.

OLD MATE MEDIA (http://oldmatemedia.com)
Chris and Kate offer professional editing services and will provide a quote upon request.

RACHEL LEIGH (https://racheleighproofreading.com)
Rachel offers proofreading and copy editing services, and charges per word.

RED PEN PROOFREADING
(https://www.redpenproofreading.com)
Caralee offers proofreading services and charges per word. She also offers rush and expedited services.

SUE COPSEY
(http://www.suecopsey.com/www.suecopsey.com/Editing.html)
Sue does content, copy, and line editing. As part of her edits, she formats files ready for print layout and ebook conversion. She covers

both fiction and non-fiction authors, and has experience with children's and YA fiction. Sue provides sample edits, along with a quote.

OTHER MARKETPLACES:

FIVERR (https://www.fiverr.com/categories/writing-translation/proofreading-editing)
Pick and choose your own proofreading and editing service among hundreds of providers.

FREELANCER (https://www.freelancer.com)
Browse hundreds of editors.

REEDSY (https://reedsy.com)
Reedsy is a marketplace full of vetted professional editors for every editing level and genre.

UPWORK (https://www.upwork.com/cat/writing)
Browse highest-rated writers and freelancers. Hourly rate.

Part II
HOW TO ILLUSTRATE YOUR FIRST CHILDREN'S BOOK

CHAPTER FIVE

ILLUSTRATIONS

This is one of the most comprehensive chapters, as it covers a hugely important topic for aspiring children's book authors. When it comes to illustrating your book, there are three choices:

ILLUSTRATION OPTIONS:
1. Do them yourself
2. Hire someone
3. Combination of both

For most self-publishing children's authors, this part of the book-creation process is the most complex and nerve-racking, because you're putting your work – your vision – into someone else's hands. More than likely it'll be a person you've never met, with whom you'll only communicate via email or over the phone.

Preparing the illustrations yourself will definitely save you money, and will keep all elements within your control. But it will also slow you down significantly, as it takes time to create a large number of illustrations. It also requires you to be somewhat talented when it comes to drawing, painting, or sketching, depending on the style you have in mind.

I have both hired an illustrator and created the illustrations myself for my books. Both have their advantages and disadvantages. Another approach is to share the workload, by hiring an illustrator for some of the work, and doing the rest yourself. However, if you do this the work must be split in such a way that all illustrations have a similar look and feel to them. For example, you will both have to use the same technique (e.g. watercolor, pencil sketch, digital). So make sure you agree on that before you hire someone.

Also, to ensure the illustrations are consistent throughout the book, you'll want to split the workload something like this: you do the illustrations where the characters/subjects are positioned in the foreground (i.e. close-ups), while your illustrator deals with the wider views/backgrounds (or vice versa).

I wouldn't recommend splitting things in such a way that one person illustrates the first five images, and the second person all the remaining images. The reader will most certainly be able to see that shift in illustration styles.

Another way you could split the workload would be to have your illustrator create the sketches or outlines of all the scenes and characters, and you add the color (or vice versa).

In order to communicate the key points to a prospective illustrator, you'll want to create an illustrator package for your book. In this chapter, we'll prepare an illustrator package and I will walk you through how to find and hire a professional illustrator, if you decide not to do the illustrations yourself.

ILLUSTRATOR BRIEFING PACKAGE
(INFORMATION TO GIVE YOUR ILLUSTRATOR IN
ADVANCE)

- The number of internal images required
- Book format (dimensions – portrait, landscape, square)
- Print book extent (number of pages)
- Whether cover art is required (in addition)
- How text and images will be combined
- RGB color profile for images (if you have a specific one in mind)
- Image resolution: 300dpi (to ensure high-enough resolution for printing)

In order to gather all we need for this illustrator package, we'll be looking at the different book/page sizes available; how to use templates, and how to create storyboards or book dummies. So let's dive right in.

ARTWORK SPECIFICATIONS

Whether you hire an illustrator or do the illustrations yourself, you'll want to make sure you do the sizing correctly, so that once you upload your artwork, everything runs smoothly.

AVAILABLE PRINT SIZES ON CREATESPACE

Createspace's available print sizes will depend on whether your book is going to be in color or black and white. Below are the most common sizes for color books. I have also included a visual size chart from Createspace.

- 5.5" x 8.5"
- 6" x 9"
- 6.14 x 9.21"
- 7" x 10"
- 8" x 10"

- 8.5" x 8.5"
- 8.5" x 11"

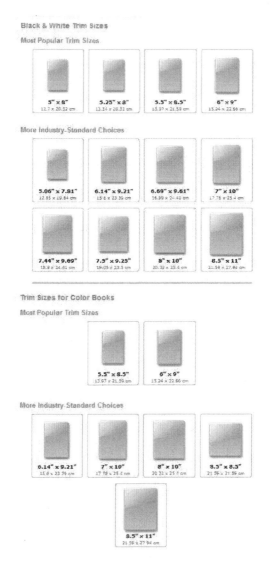

If you decide to have your illustrations cover the entire page, make sure to add 0.125 to the top, bottom, and one side edge to account for trimming! Createspace offers templates at https://forums.createspace.com/en/community/docs/DOC-1323, but remember that you'll still have to add the bleed allowance yourself.

Here is a quick example from my book *The Little Mower That Could*: Let's say you want your book to be 8.5" x 8.5":

- Add 0.125 to the top, bottom, and one side (the outside edge)
- Image size with bleed should be 8.63" x 8.75" (w x h), (or 2589 pixels x 2625 pixels at a resolution of 300 pixels/inch)
- This is only necessary for interior pages if the art covers the ENTIRE page
- This is ALWAYS necessary for the cover on ALL four sides

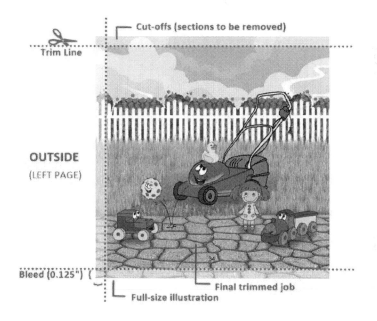

IMAGE SIZING

The larger, the better. At least 2,500 pixels per side, preferably larger. Take printing into account. For example, if your book will be 11" on one side, your images need to be more than 3,300 pixels on that side. Just make sure the aspect ratio remains the same if you should decide to resize your images.

Here's a great Inches-to-Pixels and Pixels-to-Inches converter so you know how large your image should be depending on your selected trim size. Be sure to select a DPI (Dots Per Inch) of 300.

- INCHES-TO-PIXELS:
  https://www.ninjaunits.com/converters/pixels/inches-pixels

- PIXELS-TO-INCHES:
  https://www.ninjaunits.com/converters/pixels/pixels-inches

STORYBOARD/ BOOK DUMMY

How do we decide what to include in the illustrations on each page? How can we make sure the images match up with the text?

That's where a storyboard or book dummy comes in. There are many different ways of using this technique. What follows is the way I've found works best for me. The process differs slightly between picture books and chapter books. I'll illustrate both.

> **WHY DO WE CREATE A BOOK DUMMY / STORYBOARD?**
> - Gives you a clearer vision of how the book will look.
> - Lets you see the overall flow of the story.
> - Helps you spot any potential holes in your plot.
> - Allows you to see whether or not your story makes sense.
> - Helps with the overall layout of your story so that text and illustrations match up on each page.
> - Gives you an idea of how many illustrations you need.
> - Sets the stage for hiring an illustrator.

For picture books, I usually like to work backwards. Now that you've written your story, this will be easy to do. Remember – this is not the final layout. This is just meant to help you determine what illustrations you would like to include so that you can create an illustrator brief. This step is also helpful if you are planning to create your illustrations yourself.

You already know how many pages your book will have (see your *Structure Sheet*). You'll use this information to evenly distribute the text throughout that number of pages. Let's say you have 32 pages (15 double-page spreads plus 2 single pages). It's helpful to create an actual dummy to help us with the next steps. Here's how:

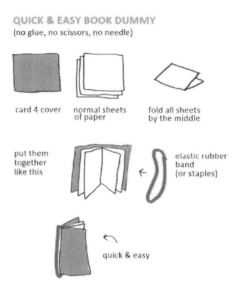

Print out your manuscript and divide the text into 15 parts. Cut them out and paste them into the actual book dummy you've created, one part per double-page spread.

Flipping through each page, read your pasted text and think of an illustration that would go nicely with that particular text; start sketching on the page opposite to your pasted text.

This storyboard creation process doesn't have to be perfect – you just want to get the essence of the story right. So be loose and expressive, and have some fun. All in all, you'll probably create a couple different versions, each being an improvement of the previous one.

I used the storyboard technique for my book *The Impatient Little Vacuum*. Below are the simple sketches I came up with for each page (depicted without the text).

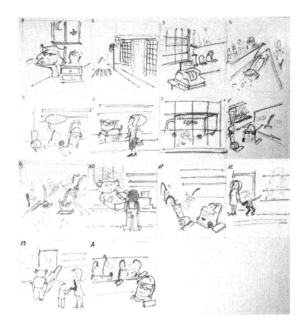

For chapter books, you won't have to use this process to determine the overall layout. I like to include at least one full illustrated page per chapter. And because each chapter automatically requires us to begin a new page, the setup is much easier.

If your chapter book has ten chapters, for example, you would want around ten illustrated pages. The theme of each illustration would depend on what happens in the corresponding chapter. Pick the most exciting part within that chapter to be illustrated, and then place that illustration where its particular scene occurs within the story. Either sketch those scenes out or describe and write down your idea.

Armed with a clear vision for each illustration, you are well on your way to creating your illustrator brief.

———————— ◆◈◆ ————————

TEXT AND ILLUSTRATION COMBINATION

How you combine your text and illustrations is really a design question and completely up to you. But because the creation process depends on your chosen combination, you will have to decide in advance so you can let your illustrator know.

There are two ways of combining text and illustrations:

1.   TEXT AS PART OF THE IMAGE
2.   TEXT AND IMAGE SEPARATE

TEXT AS PART OF THE IMAGE

Having the text in the image itself makes formatting much easier, as you don't have to worry about page breaks or font sizes. It will also look consistent across different devices.

I usually use this method for my full-color children's books. You can use whatever font you want, and the text can go anywhere on the page, making it fun and engaging for little ones' eyes.

Below (left) is a page from my book *The Garbage Trucks Are Here*, and on the right, one from my book *A Gemstone Adventure*. Here, I have added a layer underneath the text to make the text stand out.

If you decide to include the text in the image itself, this will have to be done by your illustrator. Or, if you feel your skills are up to it, you can add the text yourself once you receive the finished images, using simple graphics software.

Bear in mind that this method does make editing the text a bit harder – any changes or corrections have to be made within the image itself.

Text in illustration

Text in illustration with layer underneath

TEXT AND IMAGE SEPARATE

The other option is to have the images and text completely separate, with the text either below the illustration or on a separate page. Below is a double-page spread from my chapter book series *The Amulet Of Amser*. It has an image on the left-hand page and the text on the right-hand page.

Here, the layout would be arranged by the book formatter (or yourself), and does not involve your illustrator.

FINDING AN ILLUSTRATOR

To find the most suitable illustrator for your children's book, you should look for more than one prospective artist so that you have some choices. Having backup options in place is advisable, in case the illustrator you initially selected doesn't deliver on time or isn't able to communicate as well as you'd like.

Here's a short list of outsourcing sites:
- Upwork.com
- Guru.com
- Fiverr.com
- Freelancer.com

Social media sites (children's book specific):
- LinkedIn – artist and illustrator groups
- Facebook artist/ illustrator groups
- Goodreads groups
- DeviantArt
- ChildrensIllustrators.com

Friends and family:
- Personally, this is an option I wouldn't recommend. People tend to take illustrating less seriously if there is no or very little money involved. Usually, friends and family don't illustrate for a living, therefore it might take them a lot longer, as they are less motivated. If communication breaks down or if anything goes wrong, there could be hurt feelings and awkwardness. So be really careful if you go this route. If you do, I'd recommend paying them, as you would a third-party illustrator. That way, s/he has a real motivation and obligation. Also, make sure you have very clear deadlines and expectations put into place.

The outsourcing sites mentioned above are great, for multiple reasons. For example, most provide you with reviews from the artists' previous clients. Some even include information about previous completion rates, something I really pay attention to. And most importantly, these sites are cost effective. You have to weed through the profiles a bit, but if you find the perfect illustrator who offers the style you're going for, the research will be absolutely worth it.

WHAT TO INCLUDE IN A JOB POSTING

On most of these sites you post your project, and illustrators then bid on this. I've included swipe files that you can use to post your ↘ *Illustrator Project Description* into any of these suggested sites. It includes everything you'll want to express and has had excellent results (bids from illustrators).

> ## WHAT TO INCLUDE IN JOB POSTING:
> 1. Short project description/ what the illustrations are for
> 2. Estimated number of images
> 3. Estimated time frame/ delivery date
> 4. Placeholder price (most freelancers will bid using your offered price as an anchor)
> 5. Specify that future work is possible
> 6. Ask for portfolio
> 7. Ask for sample illustration

In order to get an idea of how much you should be offering (placeholder price), browse some of the platform's current projects. Know that your bid sets a baseline only, as each illustrator will bid individually on your project if he or she is interested in working with you.

When it comes to finding an illustrator, the key is to be proactive, rather than to wait for the perfect illustrator to find you and your posted project. Especially if you have a particular illustrator in mind.

What do I mean by proactive?

To increase engagement and bids of potential illustrators, don't just sit back and wait for the bids to come in. Instead, actively search the site and seek out illustrators whose portfolios you really like and who you believe would be a great fit for your project. Once you have uploaded your project description, ping the illustrators you like and invite them to view your project. If they agree with your set terms, they will place a bid. This proactive approach will double, if not triple the bids you'll receive. And the more bids you receive, the bigger the illustrator pool will be to choose from.

After the initial bidding process (usually a couple of days), you will have to go through each illustrator's profile and portfolio to decide who would be a great fit. The first time you go through this weeding-out process, you'll eliminate those you don't plan on hiring.

To see if an illustrator is a great fit, I recommend you go through a vetting process. I usually look at their profile and read through previous reviews, and view their portfolio to get a feel for their style. But the most important part of vetting is a sample request where you see how effectively they can turn your writings into illustrations, and how well they follow instructions.

SAMPLE ILLUSTRATION REQUEST

Once you have narrowed it down to about 6–10 illustrators, you can request a sample illustration. If you do your research and personalize your message, most are more than happy to do so. Be sure to approach at least eight, as there will always be a couple who won't respond.

I have included some swipe files for a ◥ *Sample Illustration Request*. I have also included what you could write in order to let the individual illustrators know you are still waiting on some other samples. Please be respectful of each artist's time, and the effort he or she puts into this process. If you should decide not to work with a certain talent, please let him or her know. Again, I have included a sample script you can use to do so respectfully, and without closing any doors, in case you should decide to work with the artist on another project of yours sometime in the future.

Besides helping you decide which illustrator to pick based on their artistic skills, this sample request will also help to see whether or not the illustrator is able to follow your written instructions.

Note that within the *Sample Request*, I've made a reference to the illustrator's completion rate. Depending on which platform you're using, you will be provided with an artist's completion rate, i.e. the percentage of work that a particular artist has accepted AND completed. If your project requires the artist to draw multiple images, a higher completion rate is definitely important and something to consider, as you don't want him or her to drop the project in the middle of the process. If this happened, you'd then have to find a new illustrator and would lose valuable time.

Here's an artist profile from www.freelancer.com:

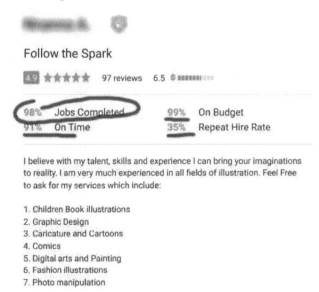

Follow the Spark

4.9 ★★★★★ 97 reviews   6.5 💲▪▪▪▪▪▪

98% Jobs Completed   99% On Budget
91% On Time   35% Repeat Hire Rate

I believe with my talent, skills and experience I can bring your imaginations to reality. I am very much experienced in all fields of illustration. Feel Free to ask for my services which include:

1. Children Book illustrations
2. Graphic Design
3. Caricature and Cartoons
4. Comics
5. Digital arts and Painting
6. Fashion illustrations
7. Photo manipulation

With a completion rate of 98% and a repeat hire rate of 35%, this is a likely candidate, depending on whether or not I like his or her actual sample illustration.

I usually illustrate my children's books myself, but for my very first chapter book, I decided to go with an illustrator.

Here are a number of sample sketches I received for one of my sample requests. My brief scene description read as follows (I've included the entire sample request email in the ⬎ *Sample Illustration Request*).

"[...] SAMPLE SCENE: black and white sketch; boy standing in driveway next to car (car door still open); time of day: dusk, right before sun is setting; boy looking curiously at house in front of him (perspective: corner of majestic house); bushes to the side; dark shadow visible behind bushes. [...]"

ILLUSTRATOR BRIEFING

As I prefer not to send the manuscript in its entirety to the illustrator, I usually prepare an illustrator brief.

An illustrator brief is meant to guide the illustrator in the creation process. Rather than going back and forth via email, you can create this set of instructions and descriptions in order to help your illustrator understand exactly what you are looking for with regards to each scene. This can be as specific or vague as you want it to be.

Your illustrator can use this briefing package to prepare a storyboard, which he or she will present to you for approval before the actual illustration process begins. Following these outlined steps will cut down on emails sent to clarify certain points, which in turn helps keep the process as simple as possible.

Besides the size, text and illustration combination, and book dummies previously discussed, most of my briefings also include sample images sourced from the web. These help the illustrator to see what exactly you are visualizing – you can attach them when you're emailing the illustrator.

ILLUSTRATOR BRIEFING PACKAGE CHECKLIST

☐ Define artwork resolution (300dpi)
☐ Desired book layout (portrait, landscape, square)
☐ RGB color profile for images (optional)
☐ Format you want all finished illustrations be delivered in
☐ Print book size
☐ The number of images
☐ Cover image (optional)
☐ Text and image combination
☐ Screenshots of sample images
☐ Storyboard with your sketches OR description of desired scenes for each image
☐ Art release form (covered below)

To make this process as easy as possible for you, I have included an ↘ *Illustrator Briefing Template* you can fill out and send to your illustrator once you've agreed to work together.

Before your illustrator begins, he or she must fill out and virtually sign an art release form. It's very important to get this in writing.

ART RELEASE FORM

When working with illustrators, you'll want to have a contract in place before they start on your project, in order to prevent any legal disputes or financial issues later on.

You will want to be the sole holder of the rights to all illustrations, and therefore you need to ensure that the contract states that all rights must be signed over to you. This will prevent any potential legal disputes and is in fact required by traditional publishers, in case your book should catch their attention. Once the work is done, the illustrations belong to you in their entirety.

I've included an ⬎ *Art Release Form Template*. Feel free to tweak it to meet your specific needs. I have used this contract for all the books I hired an illustrator for, and it has worked out well. That being said, please keep in mind that I'm not a lawyer. So be sure to have a lawyer review it to ensure all expectations have been laid out and that you're protected from a legal standpoint.

If you decide to write up your own, be sure to include the following information:

ELEMENTS OF ART RELEASE FORM
- Deadlines
- Expectations of what will be delivered (how many illustrations), in what format (raw originals, jpg, png, etc.), how (via email, shared cloud-based service, etc.) and when
- Revision policy (maximum number of revisions; guaranteed revisions, hybrid)
- Payment schedule (milestones, bonus) > see below
- Grounds of termination

If you use the recommended outsourcing sites I mentioned earlier, you won't have to worry about such a contract, as they usually take care of all these legal elements for you. However, I personally always ask my illustrator to sign such a contract, just in case.

Once the contract has been signed, you're ready to start with the actual illustration process.

◆•◆◆•◆

WHAT TO PAY & HOW TO PAY

In order to get a feel for what prices are acceptable for any given project, I recommend browsing the outsourcing site to find postings for similar projects. I'm refraining from including actual prices, as those differ greatly from service provider to service provider, and also change over time.

When hiring an illustrator via one of these outsourcing sites, payments are generally released based on milestones that you get to set. For example, you may release the first milestone payment after the storyboard has been submitted. The milestone setup will depend on the scope of your project and the platform you are using to hire your illustrator.

The cost of your illustrator depends on multiple things. First and foremost is the number of illustrations – the more you need, the more you'll pay.

The price also depends on the complexity of the artwork. Using watercolors will be more time consuming, and therefore will cost more than purely digitalized images, for example. The simpler your illustrations, the more you'll save.

Another aspect is the skill level and experience of the illustrator, as well as his or her location. Usually, artists located in Western Europe, the US, Canada, and Australia will charge more than artists in Asian or Eastern European Countries.

And finally, the pricing will depend on the delivery speed. The more quickly you require your artwork, the more it generally costs in order to move you up in the illustrator's drawing queue.

As I mentioned above, a good way to gauge the pricing is to look at similar posted projects on the particular outsourcing site you're planning to use. What are they offering? What are the offers of the bidding illustrators?

You can either pay a price per illustration, a flat fee, or a percentage.

BASIS OF PRICE
1. Price per illustration
2. Flat fee
3. Percentage of sales
4. + BONUS

PRICE PER IMAGE:

Illustrators outside the US/UK/Canada/Australia start at around US$10–20 per illustration for simple digital images. Most other styles will increase the costs.

FLAT FEE VS. PERCENTAGE OF SALES:

I recommend paying the illustrator based on a flat fee. As soon as the illustrations are done, the artwork is yours, as opposed to still being owned by the illustrator, saving you from potential legal and accounting hassles.

Providing a flat fee also gives the illustrator more motivation to complete the artwork as quickly as possible, as opposed to having an open-ended contract.

Also keep in mind that initial sales of your finished book might be quite low and slow at first, so paying your illustrator based on sales might be disappointing for them if payments trickle in rather slowly.

And once your book does take off and sells really well, it might have been cheaper to have paid a flat rate to begin with and be done with the payment.

BONUS:

Offering to pay a bonus if the project is delivered on time is a great way to ensure that your illustrator will stay on track or work even faster.

The bonus doesn't have to be big; 20–30% will do. This percentage, of course, will depend on the cost of your project, and shouldn't exceed $50.

If your illustrator delivers on time (or even ahead of schedule), do hold up your end of the bargain and pay the bonus.

––––––––––◆◦●◦◆––––––––––

MILESTONES – PAYMENT PROCESS

If you're hiring through an outsourcing site, pay through the payment options they provide. If you hire your illustrator outside of such a site, pay via PayPal or escrow.com.

SAMPLE PAYMENT SCHEDULE

MILESTONE 01:
Illustrator sends rough sketches for all pages/ storyboard
➔ Send 25% of payment (w/o bonus)
MILESTONE 02:
Illustrator sends low-resolution updates of finalized images for feedback and revisions
➔ Send 25% of payment (w/o bonus)
MILESTONE 03:
Illustrator completes full-resolution images
➔ Once all images (and cover) are complete, send remaining 50% plus bonus if applicable
➔ Illustrator sends original and high-resolution artwork.

Regular check-ins are key when working with a freelancer, as you will want to keep the delivery date on your illustrator's radar. You will also want to keep time zone differences in mind. A constant and regular update is preferable, as you don't want a bunch of work done that isn't right. If your illustrator sends you his first image, you can critique it, and he can then use those pointers for all other images. This, in turn, will save you both lots of time and nerves.

If you have a very clear vision in mind, be sure to tell your illustrator.

––––––––––◆◦●◦◆––––––––––

YOUR TO DOs FOR THIS CHAPTER:

☐ Create a book dummy
☐ Post an illustrator project with the *Illustrator Project Description Template*
☐ Request sample illustrations with the *Sample Illustration Request Template*
☐ Create illustrator briefing with the *Illustrator Briefing Template*
☐ Create art release form with the *Art Release Form Template*
☐ Set up payment milestones

Be sure to use all the lists, templates, and swipe files I've provided you with. You can find them here:

↘ http://www.eevijones.com/book-downloads

FEATURED ILLUSTRATORS

Below is a list of illustrators I have either previously worked with or who have been recommended to me by other authors. I've presented them in alphabetical order.

Please note that I am not an affiliate to any of these services. I'm not being compensated by any of these artists or service providers in any way. It's just my way of showing my appreciation for such an amazing community and is meant to spread the word about and among truly amazing people.

ABIRA DAS (https://abira-darkhues.blogspot.com)
Abira from Dark Hues has worked with authors like Sigal Adler. Contact her via abiradas.stgs@gmail.com

ANDA ANSHEEN (http://andasillustrations.daportfolio.com)
Anda creates children's books illustrations, conceptual illustrations and other related work.

DANIELA SOSA (http://danielasosa.com)
Daniela is an independent illustrator, focusing primarily on children's books.

EMINENCESYS (https://www.fiverr.com/eminencesys)
A team of experienced illustrators on Fiverr, specializing in children's book illustrations and comic books.

JEN BLOSSOM (https://www.facebook.com/blossom.jen)
Jenny is an independent illustrator.

JEN HENNING (https://jhillustration.wordpress.com/childrens-book-illustration)
Jen is capable of designing, and creatively adapting, to almost any style you as writer require.

MEGAN FRANK ILLUSTRATION (http://megan-frank-illustration.com)
Megan specializes in children's book work featuring animal characters in natural environments.

OTHER MARKETPLACES:

FIVERR (https://fiverr.com)
Pick and choose your own illustration service from hundreds of providers.

FREELANCER (https://www.freelancer.com)
Browse hundreds of illustrators.

UPWORK (https://www.upwork.com)
Browse highest-rated illustrators. Hourly rate.

CHAPTER SIX

YOUR BOOK COVER DESIGN

Before you approach any potential cover designers, you'll need to have the following ready to go:

COVER DESIGNER PACKAGE

1. Any specific illustrations from your book you wish to be included on the cover
2. Title + subtitle of your book
3. Author name, written as you want it displayed
4. * Illustrator name, if you choose to include it
5. Blurb (text) for the back of your book
6. ** Excerpts of an editorial review
7. ISBN barcode (see below)
8. Size (dimensions) of your book
9. Number of pages (this will determine the width of your spine)
10. If you have a particular design in mind, a screenshot of a similar book cover
11. A logo of your imprint, if you decide to use one (see below)

* The name of the illustrator is not a must! This, of course, is up to you, as you own all the rights for the illustrations.
** If you would like to include an excerpt of an editorial review, you would include that in the package so the cover designer can add it to the cover.

This list may seem daunting, but don't worry, I'll take you through the process of how to acquire the elements we haven't yet covered.

But first, what do you think makes a great book cover?

WHAT MAKES A GREAT COVER?

1. Needs to fit the genre and appeal to the age group.
2. * Font/s should be engaging and easily readable.
3. Colors should pop and complement each other.
4. Make sure the chosen illustration works well for the cover.
5. If you're writing a book series, make sure some of the elements on the cover remain the same from book to book so it's easily recognized as part of the series.
6. Test a thumbnail version of your cover to make sure the title is still readable and not too small.

* I've compiled a list of the ⬎ *Best Fonts For Children's Book Covers.*

Since you've selected your title already, you should have a clear idea of the message you want your book cover to bring across. Use this message to come up with a couple of concept ideas. Browsing Amazon's applicable book categories can provide you with a number of great ideas. Save those that you like and which inspire you, so you can provide your cover designer with some samples, or use them as inspiration if you design your cover yourself. You could also create Pinterest boards for your cover ideas and send the link to your designer. The designer can then add similar images for you to view. Collaboration and communication are important, so be sure to use the means that work best for you.

DIY VS. HIRING A COVER DESIGNER

Of course, it's entirely up to you whether you hire someone to create your book cover or tackle this on your own. Just remember that people really do judge a book by its cover. An intriguing and eye-catching cover is very important. You've put so much time and effort into creating your book – don't skimp on the very first thing a potential reader will see.

To illustrate my point, below are different covers from two of my earlier books. The first one is a non-fiction book, *Closing The Gap: Understanding Your Service(wo)man*. These are the three covers I went through. Would you believe that I truly, truly loved covers 1 and 2? I thought they were the best designs out there. And clearly they are NOT. It hurts my eyes just looking at them.

The same holds true for my chapter book series *The Amulet of Amser*. I'm quite embarrassed by the first two covers, which I actually used to launch this book series. Looking at these now, I'm horrified by what my brain came up with AND so willingly approved.

You truly want a polished and professional-looking cover, as this is the very first impression your potential reader will get.

If you try doing your cover yourself, especially for the first time, you *will* fall in love with whatever you create, thinking it couldn't be any better. Please listen to me: *Do not try to create your cover yourself, unless you are a professional graphic designer.* If you are, then give it a go. But if you're someone who considers Canva a good option, please rethink and leave it to an actual designer. Creating a powerful cover is an art in itself.

You should be very thorough in your choice of cover designer. Make sure his or her portfolio showcases at least a couple of children's book covers, as these differ greatly from those of other genres. If you have a specific designer in mind but can't find any samples, ask whether or not she has experience in that genre.

Before hiring a cover designer, you need to be aware that they simply *design* your cover, they don't illustrate it. If you want a specific illustration, for example showing your book's main character, you'll have to ask your illustrator to create that for you. Be sure to let him or her know that this particular piece is going to be used for the book's cover, so it can be sized accordingly.

Book your cover designer well in advance, as they are usually very busy and fill up quickly. As before, I've included a number of cover designers at the end of this chapter to help you get started with the search.

WHAT TO REQUEST FROM A COVER DESIGNER

When hiring a cover designer, you'll want to request all required formats to ensure a smooth upload of your manuscript and ebook.

1. Printed version cover
2. Cover sheet (Front/ Spine/ Back) as a PDF file
3. Ebook cover
4. 3D cover mock-up

You need to request a separate cover for your printed version and ebook, because they will differ slightly in size.

Your cover must be a single PDF that includes the back cover, spine, and front cover as one image (see photo below). Depending on your book's extent, you may or may not be able to have your title and name printed on the spine. For books with fewer than 130 pages, for example, Createspace strongly recommends a blank spine. Blank spines are required for books with less than 101 pages.

Createspace's cover specifications can be found here:

- https://www.createspace.com/Special/Enterprise/Publisher/submission_guidelines.jsp
- https://www.createspace.com/Products/Book/CoverPDF.jsp

The cover sheet below is from my book *Closing The Gap: Understanding Your Service(wo)man*.

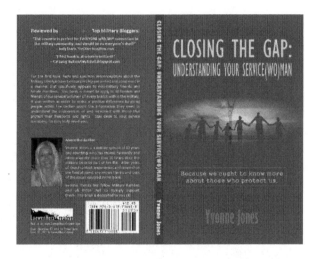

As my only non-children's book, it consists of more than 130 pages, enabling me to add the title and my name to my spine. The back holds all the elements we discussed in Chapter 3 – reviews from influencers, the actual blurb, a couple of paragraphs about the author (including an image), a logo, and the ISBN barcode.

A 3D mockup is useful for promotional purposes. Most cover designers provide them as part of their service. Here is a mockup for three of my children's books combined.

WHERE TO GET YOUR ISBN

An International Standard Book Number is a unique numeric commercial book identifier.

If you're planning to publish your book as an ebook on Amazon only, you won't need an ISBN. But if you wish to publish a paperback version, you are required to add an ISBN. When it comes to acquiring an ISBN, you have a number of different options:

ISBN OPTIONS
1. Free Createspace-assigned ISBN
2. Custom universal ISBN ($99)
3. Provide your own ISBN

The free version seems appealing. Note, however, that this Createspace-assigned ISBN will only be recognized by Createspace itself and Amazon, and issues might arise if you were ever to leave Createspace, because you can't use this ISBN to print at any other printer. Also, you'll be unable to list your own imprint as the publisher. I'll explain below what an imprint is.

However, if your ultimate goal is to make your book easily available to libraries and academic institutions, then choose option 1, as the only way you can make your book available to them is via Createspace's expanded distribution channels. These expanded channels use Ingram to get that distribution. All these books are listed as Createspace's books, as the individual authors don't have accounts at Ingram, and instead, are all rolled into one account.

Options 2 and 3 are pretty much the same. Both allow you to set a custom imprint while keeping your distribution and publishing options open.

If you're planning to write only one book, then you should choose option 2. If, however, you expect to publish more than one book further down the line, I'd recommend going with option 3 and buying the set of 10 ISBNs as a bundle, as you'll get a good discount that way.

You can purchase your ISBN either from Bowker (https://www.myidentifiers.com) or your local ISBN agency (https://www.isbn-international.org/agencies).

While I'd recommend getting your ISBN from Bowker, don't waste money on acquiring the actual barcode from them. You can get this completely free from this fantastic barcode generator (http://bookow.com/resources.php).

A barcode on your printed book is required by most of the largest book retailers as well as wholesalers, and since you can get them for free, you should include one on your book's cover. This screenshot illustrates the specifications I suggest. Click on the *"email.PNG barcode"* button and you'll have your barcode emailed to you in no time at all.

Just remember, people really do judge a book by its cover. And if your book cover design doesn't follow these important guidelines, your book – no matter how well written – will fail.

IMPRINT

An imprint is a trade name under which you can publish your work. It allows authors to establish a brand identity, especially if they have written (or plan on writing) more than one book.

A senior analyst at Bowker I talked to explained an imprint as follows:

> "An imprint is a trade name used by a publisher to identify a line of books or a publishing arm within the publishing organization. ... An imprint is distinguished from a corporate name in that it does not represent an entity with a corporate life of its own."

The imprint I've used for all of my books is LHC Publishing, which is part of my motion graphics studio, LoewenHerz-Creative (http://loewenherz-creative.com).

If you decide to create your own imprint, you'll have to make sure that your imprint you listed at Bowker when you purchased your ISBN(s) matches the imprint you are using at Createspace, as Createspace will check your account at Bowker during the review process.

YOUR TO DOs FOR THIS CHAPTER:

- ☐ Put together your cover designer package
- ☐ List of *Best Fonts For Children's Book Covers*
- ☐ Acquire your ISBN
- ☐ Create an ISBN-13 barcode

Be sure to use all the lists, templates, and swipe files I've provided you with. You can find them here:

↘ http://www.eevijones.com/book-downloads

FEATURED COVER DESIGNERS

Below is a list of cover designers I have either previously worked with or who have been recommended to me by other authors. I've presented them in alphabetical order.

Please note that I am not an affiliate to any of these services. I'm not being compensated by any of these artists or service providers in any way. It's just my way of showing my appreciation for such an amazing community and is meant to spread the word about and among truly amazing people.

CWINEY (https://www.fiverr.com/cwiney)
Cwiney is a professional graphic designer offering ebook/ Kindle cover designs on Fiverr.

HAPPY SELF PUBLISHING
(http://happyselfpublishing.com/book-covers)
HSP followed my instructions to a tee when I had this book's cover designed. Jyotsna and her team will take great care of you.

JEN HENNING (https://jhillustration.wordpress.com/childrens-book-illustration)
Jen at JH Illustration offers cover designs for children's books.

PREMADE COVERS

BOOK COVER ZONE (https://bookcoverzone.com)
Book Cover Zone offers both premade and custom made covers.

THE BOOK COVER DESIGNER
(https://thebookcoverdesigner.com/product-category/premade-book-covers/childrens)
The Book Cover Designer is a collective of various cover designers who offer a number of premade covers for children's books.

THE COVER COLLECTION
(http://www.thecovercollection.com)
Note that the children's book section will be phased out.

OTHER MARKETPLACES

99 DESIGNS (https://99designs.com)

DEVIANT ART (http://www.deviantart.com)
An online community where artists post their work. Find an artist
whose style you like, and contact them about your book.

FIVERR (https://www.fiverr.com)
Pick and choose your own cover design service from among
hundreds of providers.

FREELANCER (https://www.freelancer.com)
Browse hundreds of cover designers.

UPWORK (https://www.upwork.com)
Browse highest-rated cover designers.

REEDSY (https://reedsy.com)
Reedsy is a marketplace full of vetted professional designers for every
level and genre.

Part III
HOW TO FORMAT, UPLOAD, AND PUBLISH YOUR FIRST CHILDREN'S BOOK

CHAPTER SEVEN

BOOK FORMATTING, ASSEMBLY & UPLOADING

There are five main book formats.

> ### MOST POPULAR BOOK FORMATS:
>
> 1. Paperback
> 2. Hardcover
> 3. Ebook
> 4. Board Book
> 5. Audio Book

This chapter will cover the formatting and uploading process for the paperback and ebook versions.

Many aspiring children's authors ask whether or not they should consider printing their book as a board book, for 0–3-year-olds. This, of course, is entirely up to you. Just note that Createspace doesn't as yet offer this option. My resource list at the end of this chapter lists a number of board book printers.

Formatting is one of my favorite stages of the entire book creation process, because this is when you see everything come together for the very first time.

There are many beautiful templates available that enable quick and easy DIY formatting for your book. And software, such as Scrivener or Vellum, allows authors to easily create the ebook version of their book. However, because picture books and chapter books include illustrations, and often many different fonts, some of the great options available to authors working in other genres aren't available to children's authors, or simple won't work. And that's why you'll have to decide whether or not to hire a professional book formatter.

The book formatting process is entirely separate from the editing process. While editing takes care of everything written, the book formatting will work on the overall look of your book, the placement of the text and illustrations, and any other esthetics that are important to make your book look as professional as possible.

If you plan on hiring a book designer (both for paper and ebook), you won't have to worry too much about the layout, as he or she will know all the required specifications for your desired book size and style.

WHAT WILL A FORMATTER DO?

Book formatters prepare your book for printing or for ebook according to the guidelines of the site you'll be submitting to.

They will put all of the text and images in the appropriate place so it prints properly or appears correctly in an ebook. They'll also arrange the front matter and back matter of the book, and will insert headers, footers, and page numbers.

A book formatter will also insert your clickable table of contents and any other links throughout your ebook version.

I have included a number of reputable book formatters at the end of this chapter. When hiring a professional formatter, make sure that he or she has some experience with children's books, either by asking directly or by going through his or her portfolio.

That being said, I formatted all my books (both ebook and paper version) myself. It took a couple of tries, but I'm glad I learned the process.

If you do decide to do your own formatting, be patient with yourself, as this will involve some trial and error to put everything together the way you want it. But once learned, it's a skill you can use over and over again if you should decide to write more than one book.

PAPERBACK FORMATTING & UPLOADING

When formatting and setting up my children's books, I usually start with my paperback, and while I'm waiting for my proof copy to arrive in the mail, I set up and upload my ebook version. Doing so allows me to complete both versions simultaneously, so that I can launch them together.

Doing it in this order also ensures that the paperback and ebook are linked automatically on Amazon, so both versions appear together on one screen when presented to potential buyers.

In Chapter 5, you decided on your book's size and downloaded a Createspace template. (If you haven't downloaded the template yet, please go ahead and do so now because it simplifies the following steps https://forums.createspace.com/en/community/docs/DOC-1323). Please note that the templates do not accommodate bleed, so you will have to alter your margins yourself once you open up the template.

If you don't want to use a Createspace template, that's fine too, as I'll show you below how to set up your own.

As the setups for picture books and chapter books differ slightly from each other, I have created two separate illustrations, one for each.

These show you the overall layout of the paper version of your book, illustrating the sequence of the contents. They show you exactly which pages to leave blank, and where to start your page numbers.

When you start working on the ebook version, you simply take out all blank pages and the page numbers. Otherwise, the setups for both formats are fairly similar, apart from any linked text and animated content.

PICTURE BOOKS – LAYOUT

Let's look at picture books first. Note that all left-hand pages have even numbers, and all right-hand pages have odd numbers. Whether or not you want to include page numbers is entirely up to you, but books for very little ones usually omit them. If you do include them, be sure that even though the title page is technically page 1, you don't start including actual page numbers until page 2.

CHAPTER BOOKS – LAYOUT

Chapter books are different, in that their page count begins at a different place. As most have a table of contents, page numbers have to be included. Note that we don't start page 1 until we get to the actual text of our book. Also note that while picture books don't include the author's name and the book's title at the top of the page (known as the "running head"), these can be included in a chapter book. But again, that is entirely up to you, as many authors and publishers prefer to leave them out to provide for a cleaner and less cluttered look.

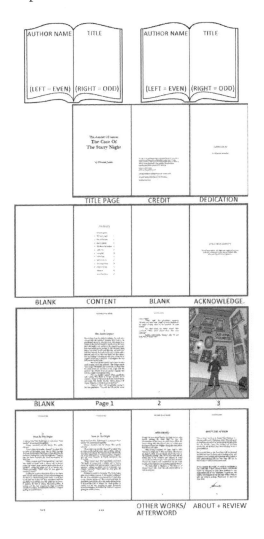

COPYRIGHT PAGE

A copyright page usually appears at the beginning of a book (both paperback and ebook) and holds the copyright notice, edition information, publication information, legal notices, and the book's ISBN or identification number. If you have an imprint, you would include its logo here as well. The dedication is often placed on the copyright page too.

Quick disclaimer: I'm not a lawyer, so please keep this in mind as you read this content pertaining to the copyright page.

The single most important element on the copyright page is the copyright notice itself. It usually consists of three elements:

1. The © symbol, or the word "Copyright"
2. The year of first publication
3. An identification of the owner of the copyright (e.g. your name)

Combining all three elements, a book I published in the year 2017 would have this:

© 2017 Y. Eevi Jones

Including a reservation-of-rights paragraph is important as well, as this is where you outline what rights you reserve and which you allow.

Putting all pieces together, you would end up with a copyright page similar to this (make sure to insert your own information in the template below):

YOUR BOOK TITLE by **YOUR NAME.** Published by
NAME OF IMPRINT / PUBLISHER.

www.YOURWEBSITE/PUBLISHERWEBSITE.COM

No part of this publication may be reproduced in whole or in part, or stored in a retrieval system, or transmitted in any form or by any means, electronic, mechanical, photocopying, recording, or otherwise, without written permission of the publisher / author. For information regarding permission, write to **INSERT PUBLISHER'S EMAIL ADDRESS / AUTHOR'S EMAIL ADDRESS.**

ISBN-10: ....
ISBN-13: ....

Text & illustration copyright © **YEAR** by **NAME.**
Cover by **COVER DESIGNER.**

Writing a copyright page isn't complicated. Simply pick the elements that seem most suitable to your book.

Now that you have set up the basics, you can dive into setting up your book for print using one of Createspace's templates.

SETTING UP THE INTERIOR OF YOUR PRINT VERSION

During the illustration chapter, we looked at whether or not your images would extend all the way to the end of the page (full bleed), or if you prefer to keep white margins along the edges of each page.

I prefer using Microsoft Word to set up my paperback interiors, simply because it's easy, and because Createspace's templates are provided as Word documents. Alternatively you can use Adobe InDesign, Mac's Pages, or Google Docs online.

The templates you download are set up for books with margins. If you wish to extend your artwork to the end of the page (full bleed), you'll have to slightly alter the template's settings by adding 0.125 to one outside edge of the page, and to the top and bottom. Opening up your page settings, you would also set the margin to zero on all sides. For an 8.5 x 8.5 inch book, for example, this would look as follows:

WIDTH: 8.5 + 0.125 = 8.63   **(outside edge only)**
HEIGHT: 8.5 + (0.125 x 2) = 8.75   **(top & bottom)**

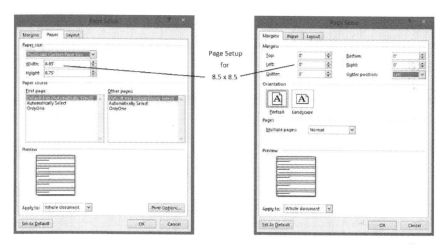

If you remember, this is also the size of artwork we requested from our illustrator. Matching our images with the page size guarantees a high-quality, high-resolution image – the quality could potentially be reduced if the illustrations needed to be resized.

Now we're ready to insert our text and images.

INSERTING OUR TEXT & IMAGES

Your book contains separate sections (e.g. title page, dedication page, etc.), so you will have to work section by section, to copy and paste your text and insert your images individually. This will ensure the page size and margins remain consistent throughout the book.

The beauty and simplicity of formatting the paperback is that it will be printed exactly as you see it. There won't be any of the surprises, such as unexpected line breaks, that you might experience with the setup of the ebook version.

Also with the paperback, you can use whatever fonts you like, as these are automatically embedded into the PDF file at the end of the conversion process.

As we are only discussing the book's interior right now, we won't include the front and back covers. These will be uploaded to Createspace separately.

Following the page layout I provided you with above, begin copying and pasting your text, page for page, resizing and repositioning as desired. For picture books, make sure the first page remains blank. Insert a "page break" whenever you want to start a new page.

Add images using the "insert picture" instruction, rather than copy and paste, as copy and pasting can reduce an image's quality. Because our page size and image size are the same, it will plug right in. Right-clicking on the image, ensure that its layout option is set to "in line with text" so that it remains where it's meant to be during the entire formatting process.

Again, remember that the pages will alternate between left (even pages) and right (odd pages).

Once you have completed the setup and have inserted all your text and images, you simply save your document as a PDF. Be sure to include the document's current settings by selecting the "document properties" within the options section, as you are selecting "PDF" as the "save as type."

UPLOADING YOUR BOOK ONTO CREATESPACE

Before we get started on uploading your book, I want to mention that the likelihood of your book coming back with listed formatting errors will be quite high, especially if this is your first time. Don't let this discourage you; simply correct the errors and upload it again.

1. First, go to https://www.createspace.com and create a new account.
2. Click on **"Add New Title"** within the member dashboard.
3. Insert the **book title** you decided on in Chapter 3, select **"Paperback,"** and select **"Guided"** as your setup process.

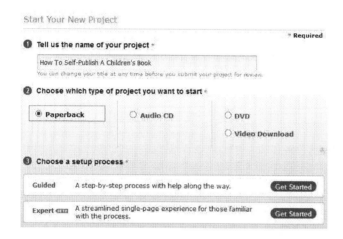

4. Insert all the required title information. Leave the publication date blank. If you choose to add your illustrator's name, you can do so by selecting "Illustrated by" from the "Add Contributors" dropdown menu. Subtitle and Series Title are both optional. **Save and Continue.**

5. Select "Provide Your Own ISBN" and enter the ISBN you purchased in Chapter 6. Insert an imprint, if you have one. Click **"Assign This ISBN."**

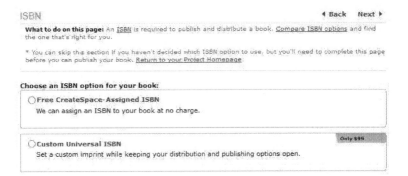

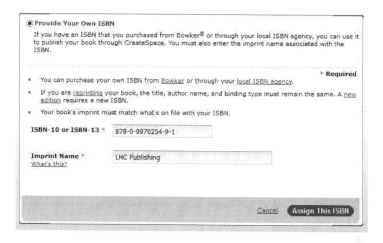

6. Choose "Full Color" and select the size for your book by clicking **"Choose a Different Size."** Upload the PDF you created in the previous section. Make sure your PDF doesn't contain the cover, as this will be uploaded separately. Uploading your interior file will take a few moments, then the Automated Print Check will start. As I said, the likelihood that it comes back error-free is pretty low, especially if this is your first time. After completion of this automated check, click on **"Launch Interior Reviewer"** to view the interior. If it looks okay, move on to the next step.

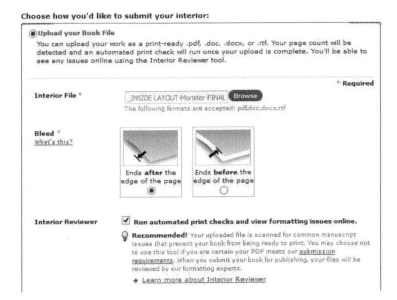

7. Select your preferred finish for your book cover. I usually choose **"Glossy"** for my children's book covers. Choose **"Upload a Print-Ready PDF Cover"** and upload your cover sheet. **Save.**

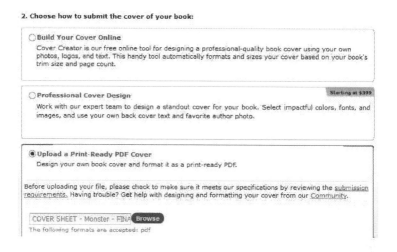

8. The next screen will ask you to **"Submit Files for Review."** Go ahead and submit your files, as it will take Createspace one or two days to review.

9. While you are waiting, you can set up the distribution channels. Here, you can choose between standard and expanded distribution. Feel free to pick whatever feels right for your circumstances. I usually just stick with the standard distribution, as it's the simplest and most cost-effective option. If in doubt, ask yourself if you are willing to call bookstores and ask them to stock your book so it's available for sale within that particular store. If not, then choosing the expanded distribution wouldn't make sense. It's also important to note that using the expanded distribution will make your book more expensive, meaning you will have to extend that increased cost to your book buyers by increasing your prices, or take a cut in your overall profit. Choosing expanded distribution channels will also limit some of Createspace's offered sizes you can choose from.

Standard Distribution FREE

✓ Selected → Amazon.com*
What's this?

✓ Selected → Amazon Europe*
What's this?

* Your Amazon site detail page should be built 3-5 business days after your title is made available for sale. Changes to your title, including list price, may take 3-5 business days to appear on Amazon sites.

10. Next, you will be asked to set up your list price. Createspace will provide you with the minimum list price for your book, meaning whatever you charge in addition to this will be your profit or royalty. As stated within a previous chapter, be sure to price your book competitively. As you are a new author, it would be hard to successfully charge premium prices, so look at the pricing of similar titles and set your list price accordingly. I usually set my price $1.50–$2.00 higher than the minimum list price for my paperbacks. Createspace will automatically generate the prices for other currencies.

List Price	Channel	Royalty
$ [ ] USD* Calculate	Amazon.com	–
Minimum list price for this title is $6.09 What's this?	Expanded Distribution ⊘ Not selected · Select Channels	

11. Next, you will be asked to add a description for your book. Here, you'll use the description you prepared in Chapter 3. Instead of simply inserting plain text, Createspace lets you use limited HTML. Kindlepreneur has an excellent description generator tool that lets you format your text and generates a code that you then simply copy and paste into Createspace (https://kindlepreneur.com/amazon-book-description-generator).

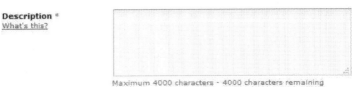

Description *
What's this?

Maximum 4000 characters · 4000 characters remaining
Advanced users can use limited HTML instead of plain text to style and format their description

Remember that a book cover blurb for children's books should be relatively short (around 200–250 words). And be sure to include your target age group and any upcoming work, especially if it's a series.

12. We get to choose one BISAC category (Book Industry Standards and Communications). These categories are used by the book-selling industry to help identify and group books by their subject matter. Choose the BISAC category that best fits your book.

BISAC Category *
What's this?

Juvenile Fiction / Transportation / Cars & Trucks   [Choose...]

➔ **Enter a BISAC code**

13. You'll also be asked to enter your author biography and the keyword phrases you researched and prepared in Chapter 3. You can enter up to five keyword phrases (each up to 25 characters long), so use them wisely, as they will help your audience find your book a lot more easily if chosen well. Remember to research them using Amazon's search bar. Don't just use single words, use phrases that people are likely to enter into the search bar when looking for a book like yours.

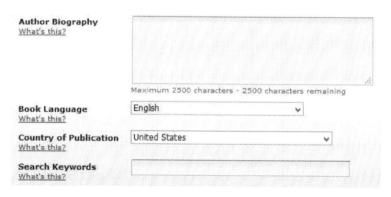

Author Biography
What's this?

Maximum 2500 characters - 2500 characters remaining

Book Language
What's this?
English

Country of Publication
What's this?
United States

Search Keywords
What's this?

14. The next screen will provide you with the option of publishing your work on KDP as an ebook. Before you can do so, you first have to create your ebook version, using the steps outlined in the section below.

15. When Createspace sent you an email telling you your files are good to go, I'd highly recommend you order a proof copy, to see how it looks in print.

Congratulations! You just completed the setup for your paperback. While you're waiting for Createspace to approve your book files, and for your printed proof copy, you can get to work formatting your ebook.

———◆◆◈◆◈———

It's important to note that KDP now also offers the printing of a paperback. I personally still stick with Createspace for the paperback, as it has a number of advantages over opting to print your paperback with KDP. However, this might change in the near future.

PAPERBACK		
AVAILABLE FEATURES	**CS**	**KDP**
Payout schedule	30 days	60 days
Wholesale author copies available	Y	N
Physical print proofs available	Y	N
Expanded distribution available	Y	N
Professional publishing services available	Y	N
Keeps old version up until new one is approved	N	Y
Available in Canada	Y	N
Available in Japan	N	Y

———◆◆◈◆◈———

EBOOK FORMATTING & UPLOADING

Ebooks aren't the main medium used by smaller children and their parents yet, but their usage has been consistently growing. The majority of parents prefer their kids to read print books, but the number of parents who prefer ebooks or who have no preference is increasing. In fact, 40% of children's book purchasers say they read ebooks to their kids.

If you haven't thought about creating an ebook version for your book, I strongly suggest you do so. As previously mentioned, paperbacks still make up the majority of my sales, but the ebook comes in handy during promotions and for review requests, which will be further discussed within the marketing section of this book. Giving away review copies using this format is a lot easier and more cost effective than sending out paperbacks.

There are multiple ways you can format the ebook version of your book, the most common ones being (1) KDP Kids Book Creator, (2) the open source formatting software Sigil, and (3) your regular Word document.

Below I have outlined the pros and cons of each method.

KDP KIDS BOOK CREATOR	SIGIL	WORD DOC
Tool for authors to turn their illustrated children's books into great-looking Kindle books	A multi-platform EPUB ebook editor. An open source software that has been developed by and for the user community	Use regular Word Doc or Google Docs - Slides
PROS		
Free Easy to learn Can add text popups Able to upload your own font	Free For Windows, Linux, Mac Able to add hyperlinks Allows you to resize images Able to upload own font	Free if you have Microsoft Office Able to add hyperlinks Able to use your own fonts

CONS

Have to download free software	Somewhat of a learning curve	Must resize image prior to inserting it into document
Can't add hyperlinks to ebook (won't be able to have clickable call to action, like reviewing your book, or link to your website)	Have to download open-source software	No popups
	No popups	
Does not allow you to resize images; must resize image prior to uploading it		
https://kdp.amazon.com/en_US/kids	https://www.techspot.com/downloads/5797-sigil.html	

SETTING UP THE INTERIOR OF YOUR EBOOK VERSION

It's important to mention that I prefer using the free open-source software Sigil. Once you've used it a couple of times, it becomes very intuitive. I prefer it over the other methods because I have more control. I can resize images within the program, and can add hyperlinks, which I believe to be a very important feature since we want people to be able to click through either to your website, or to your book on Amazon to leave a review.

Below are the steps I take when formatting my ebooks.

1. After the download, open up the Sigil software. This is the screen you will see.

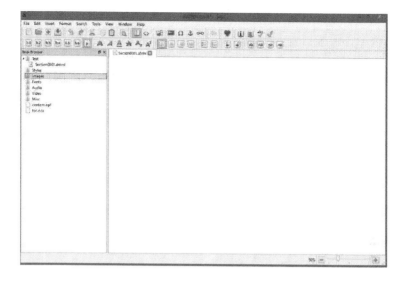

2. First, you will upload all your images into the program. All images must be in .jpg format. In the column to the left, click once on the "**Image**" folder. Once selected, right-click it and choose "**Add Existing Files.**" Find the folder that holds all your images. To select more than one image, hold the CTRL key down as you are selecting each image. After uploading all your images, you can double-click your image folder within Sigil and it will display all uploaded images.

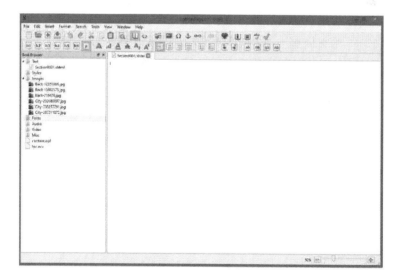

3. Copy and paste your text from your title page into the field to the right. Use Sigil's different headings settings and font sizes to format your text.

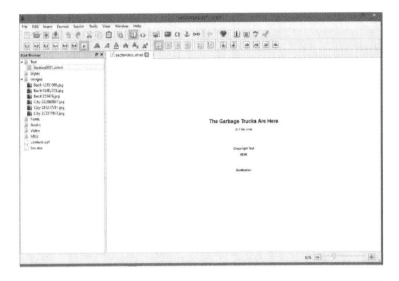

4. This first part (your title page) has been automatically named **"Section 0001.xhtml"** (see column to the left). Right-clicking that name will allow you to rename it. Using a better name (e.g. "Title Page") will help you navigate through those pages more easily once the browser is filled with many more.

5. Also note that you can flip back and forth between the regular **Book View** (which displays files in your book as they will appear to readers) and the **Code View**, which allows you to edit the formatting codes.

Book View

Code View

6. To begin a new page (or new section) in your book, be sure to place the cursor after the last word or image, click "**Edit**," then "**Split At Cursor**." This will add another section which you can then rename again, as before. Copy and paste desired text into the new section.

7. To add an image, place and click your cursor in the text area, then click "**Insert**" then "**File**." This will open up a box that holds all your previously uploaded images. Select the image you want for this particular section, then click "**Okay**." Once the image is inserted, click it and then select the **"Center"** button in the menu bar to ensure your image displays in the center of the e-reading device.

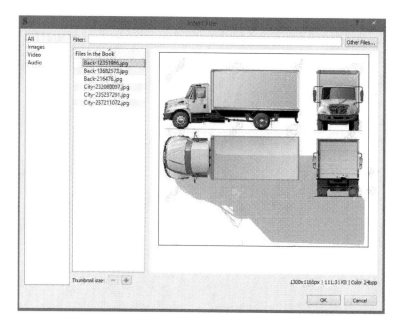

8. **IMPORTANT:** This is the only part that's a bit tricky. When inserting images, you want to make sure that the entire image fits on the screen of the e-reader device. To do so, you will have to go into the "**Code View**" (see Step 5 above), and insert **width="100%"** after the jpg entry. Here is a before and after screenshot of what this line is supposed to look like.

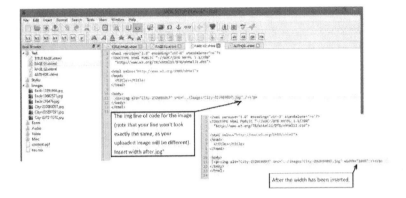

9. To hyperlink a text, highlight the text, then click on the "**Insert Link**" button in the top menu and input your URL in the bottom bar, titled "**Target.**"

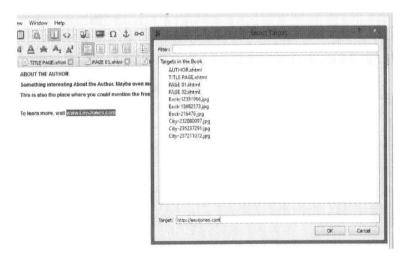

10. Save the file. Sigil will automatically save it as an .epub file. Although Kindle books are in .mobi format, you can still upload your .epub file, as KDP will convert it for you without changing any formatting.

Congratulations! You just created an amazing ebook file all on your own. And it didn't cost you a dime. Next, you will upload your file onto KDP.

UPLOADING YOUR EBOOK FILE ONTO KDP

1. First, go to http://kdp.amazon.com and create a new account. If you already have an Amazon account, you will be using this account to sign in.

2. Once you have created your KDP account, go back to Createspace where you left off after you uploaded your paperback files. Remember that you want to connect the paperback and ebook versions right away, so doing it via Createspace is the easiest way. Go back to the step within Createspace where you were provided with the option of publishing your work on KDP as an ebook.

    Once there, select **"Resubmit my files to KDP."** Doing so will automatically take the files you submitted for the paperback and convert them into KDP's ebook format, .mobi.

    Generally, we don't want to keep these automatically converted files, as the formatting is not properly set. You are simply taking this step for now in order to "link" the paperback with your ebook, so that both versions show up together once available within Amazon. Once you've been redirected to KDP, you'll upload the ebook file you just created.

3. Information like the book title and the author's name should have automatically been transferred. Go through this information to make sure everything is correct. KDP's description field does not allow HTML, so you might have to take out all the coding you previously generated at Kindlepreneur and copy and paste in the plain text.

4. Check **"I own the copyright and I hold the necessary publishing rights."**

    ⦿ I own the copyright and I hold the necessary publishing rights. What are publishing rights? ▾

    ◯ This is a public domain work. What is a public domain work? ▾

5. KDP lets you enter seven keyword phrases, two more than Createspace. Again, use the keyword phrases you prepared and researched in Chapter 3. As before, one very effective way to research them is by using Amazon's search bar. Don't just use single words; instead go for phrases that people are likely to enter into the search bar when looking for a book like yours.

6. Next, you enter your categories. KDP lets you select two. Precise browse categorization helps readers find your book, so be sure to select the most appropriate categories for your book. This, again, requires some research up front. To get an idea about what categories might work for you, look for books similar to yours and find out their categories.

    Go as deep as possible into the subcategories, so you pick spots where your book is relevant but the number of books competing in that category is small. This means your potential ranking will be higher.

7. Add the Age Range and U.S. Grade range. Both are optional, but don't take much time to fill out. Adding these can be beneficial if the potential buyer goes into specific age or grade ranges in order to find a book.

8. Select **"I'm ready to release my book now"** and hit **Save and continue**. Don't worry; selecting this option doesn't mean you have to publish your book this very moment.

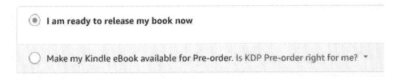

9. I usually select **"no"** for digital rights management. Some authors want to encourage readers to share their work, and choose not to have DRM applied to their book.

Digital Rights Management (DRM)

Enable DRM on this Kindle eBook. How is my Kindle eBook affected by DRM? ▾

○ Yes

◉ No

10. Next, you are asked to upload your ebook file, so go ahead and submit what you created and saved earlier.

11. Upload your ebook cover image in the .jpg format. Be sure your cover image has at least 1000 pixels on the longest side.

12. Select the **"Launch Previewer"** to see what your files look like. The launch previewer lets you view your book on multiple devices. Once you have clicked through all the pages, go back to the setup screen by clicking **"Book Details"** in the upper left-hand corner.

Online Previewer
The Online Previewer is the easiest way to preview. It lets you preview most books as they would appear on Kindle e-readers, tablets and phones.

Launch Previewer

Downloadable Preview Options
If you would like to preview your book on Kindle Touch or Kindle DX, you will want to use the downloadable previewer.
▸ Preview on your computer
▸ Preview on your Kindle device

13. Now go ahead and enter an ISBN, if you so choose. I usually leave this one blank. But do enter your imprint in the **"Publisher"** field if you did this for your paperback.

ISBN (Optional)
Kindle eBooks are not required to have an ISBN. What is an ISBN? ▾

Publisher (Optional)

14. Whether or not you enroll your book into KDP Select is completely up to you. There are many advantages in doing so, but it's important to know all the benefits and drawbacks in order to make an informed decision. Just know that this decision is not final. You can enroll at any time, and once the 90 days are up, you can un-enroll again as well. I will talk more about this option in the marketing section of this book.

BENEFITS:	Free Promotion	-You can give your book away for free up to 5 days out of the 90 days enrollment period (days don't have to be consecutive) -Great to get reviews, lead readers to other books, or build mailing list.
	Kindle Countdown	-Lets you offer time-sensitive deals on your book -Listed separately in the Kindle store, so Amazon is driving traffic for you -Creates a sense of urgency among buyers -Up to a week in a 90-day period
DRAWBACKS:	Exclusivity	-You can only sell your ebook on Amazon for those 90 days

15. Select all territories.

Select the territories for which you hold distribution rights. Learn more about distribution rights.

⦿ **All territories (worldwide rights)** What are worldwide rights? ▾

◯ **Individual territories** What are Individual Territory rights? ▾

16. The next step asks you to select a royalty plan and set the list price for your ebook. The pricing on KDP is different from Createspace, in that Createspace tells you the minimum you

will need to charge. Anything extra charged by you will make up your royalty, and combined it makes up your book's price in its print version.

KDP's pricing, however, is divided into two royalty tiers:

35%	Any price below $2.99 and above $9.99
70%	Book must be priced between $2.99 - $9.99

This pricing structure is designed to ensure that the majority of books are being sold within a specific price range.

The minimum price on KDP is $0.99. You want to price your book in such a way that you can be competitive with others, but still earn maximum commission, so be sure to check out the pricing of some of your competitors.

17. Since you will be offering a paperback version of your book, enrolling it into Kindle MatchBook may be worth considering. This gives the book buyer the opportunity to buy the Kindle version for a reduced price, if they purchase the print version first.

Enroll in Kindle MatchBook (Optional)

Give customers who purchase your print book from Amazon the option to purchase your Kindle eBook for $2.99 or less. Learn more about Matchbook.

☐ Enroll my book in Kindle MatchBook

18. The next option asks you whether or not you want to allow users to lend the ebook they have just purchased. Each book can be lent once for a duration of 14 days. During this time, the book will not be readable by the lender. I usually don't select this option.

Allow Kindle Book Lending (Optional)

Allow your customers to lend your Kindle eBook after purchasing it to their friends and family for a duration of 14 days. Learn more about Kindle Book Lending.

☐ Allow lending for this book

19. And that concludes the setup of the ebook version of your book. Congratulations! You did so, so well! All that is left for you to do is click the **"Publish Your Kindle Ebook"** button. But you don't want to do that just yet, as you're still waiting for the paperback proof to arrive. While you're waiting, you can go ahead and create a marketing plan, which we'll discuss in the next chapter.

YOUR TO DOs FOR THIS CHAPTER:

☐ Format your paperback
☐ Upload your paperback
☐ Order proof copy of your paperback
☐ Format your ebook
☐ Upload your ebook
☐ CELEBRATE!

Be sure to use all the lists, templates, and swipe files I've provided you with. You can find them here:

↘ http://www.eevijones.com/book-downloads

FEATURED BOOK FORMATTING SERVICES

Below is a list of formatting services and other resource providers that I have either previously worked with or have had recommended to me by other authors. I've presented them in alphabetical order.

Please note that I am not an affiliate to any of these services. I'm not being compensated by any of these artists or service providers in any way. It's just my way of showing my appreciation for such an amazing community and is meant to spread the word about and among truly amazing people.

EBOOK & PAPERBACK FORMATTING

CHARAKH DESIGN
https://www.fiverr.com/charakh

EBOOK LAUNCH (Print & Ebook)
https://ebooklaunch.com/ebook-formatting

INDIE DESIGNZ
http://indiedesignz.com/book-formatting-services

ISTVAN SZABO
https://www.fiverr.com/istvanszaboifj

JD SMITH – JDSMITH DESIGN (Print)
http://www.jdsmith-design.com/formatting

JEN BLOSSOM
https://www.fiverr.com/jenny_fiver

JEN HENDERSON – WILD WORDS FORMATTING
http://www.wildwordsformatting.com

MAGDALENA ROGIER - INDIE BOOK DESIGNER (Print)
http://www.indiebookdesigner.com

SARAH BILLINGTON – BILLINGTON MEDIA (Editor & Designer)
http://www.billingtonmedia.com

BOARD BOOKS

https://www.pintsizeproductions.com
http://www.printninja.com/printing-products/board-book-printing
https://www.starprintbrokers.com/portfolio/childrens-board-books

PAPERBACK

https://www.createspace.com

HARDCOVER

https://www.bookbaby.com/hardcover-book-printing
http://www.ingramspark.com
https://www.lightning-press.com
https://www.lulu.com

OTHER RESOURCES

KINDLEPRENEUR – DESCRIPTION GENERATOR TOOL
https://kindlepreneur.com/amazon-book-description-generator

IRFANVIEW – FREE GRAPHIC VIEWER & FORMATTING TOOL (Resize images)
http://www.irfanview.com/main_download_engl.htm

FINDING RIGHT CATEGORIES

SHERI FARLEY (Sheri is an Amazon Category Hunter. She searches for optimal categories for successful launches and long term sales. categoryhunter@outlook.com + phone number 816-304-3235)
https://www.facebook.com/golifemobile

Part IV
HOW TO MARKET
YOUR FIRST CHILDREN'S
BOOK

CHAPTER EIGHT

PUBLISHING & MARKETING

You did it! You've written and illustrated your book, formatted the paperback and ebook version, and uploaded both onto their hosting platforms. You should be so, so proud of yourself for all these amazing accomplishments. Now it's time to reach out and get your book noticed.

Here, you'll need to be proactive. A lot of authors just want to write and don't want to market. But without promoting your book, it will get lost in the sea of books. You have to really push for it. Even traditional publishers have to do so. If you believe in your book, then you'll fight for it.

Don't be shy when it comes to promoting your book. It's important you let others know about it. Just remember, your friends and family want to support you. They want to see you succeed. Seeing someone write and publish a book is actually very exciting to them. This is where you can and should leverage your connections.

Now it's time to prepare for your launch, which will entail the actual publishing and marketing of your book.

In this chapter we'll create a marketing plan so that we can ensure a successful launch for your book. This marketing plan will focus on three areas:

1. Organizing a Launch Team
2. Reviews
3. Promotions
4. BONUS: Influencer Reviews

ORGANIZING A LAUNCH TEAM

First off, you will want to form what is called a "launch team." This means you are going to organize all the people you think would be interested in your book and who would be willing to help you. Such people could include your family and friends, acquaintances, and colleagues.

There are a number of reasons why you want a launch team. First, they'll help you spread the word about your new book, either via word of mouth or through social media, such as Facebook. Second, they'll provide you with your very first reviews, which are extremely important, as they are social proof and let others know about the value of your book, so you can sell even more. And third, your launch team members' downloads following the launch will help with your book's ranking on Amazon. In short, a launch team provides you with a great initial boost.

Members of your launch team have early access to a copy of your book, and agree to post a review once it's been published. I generally advise authors to provide their launch team with a short summary of the book (and/or chapter summaries), as many people might not have the time to read the entire book. Children's books, however, are a bit different, since they are generally pretty short and therefore a summary isn't usually necessary. Instead, you can let team members know specifically how long (short) your book is, so they know what to expect.

Your social media launch request could be shared via places like Facebook, LinkedIn, or simply sent via email, and could look something like this:

"*** EXCITING NEWS ***

Dear friends and family! I am sooo excited to announce that I'm about to publish my very first children's book, *The Garbage Trucks Are Here*. It has truly been a labor of love and I cannot wait to share it with you!

I would so love your help with the launch of my book by becoming a member of my Launch Team. As a member, you would get early access to my book; and if you love it, would post an honest review on Amazon once I officially launch the book.

With 17 illustrated double-pages, it's a super quick and fun read for 2-5 year-olds, rhyming and roaRRRing its way through the streets!

Five hungry garbage trucks come to town to gobble up all the trash and waste they can find. It's a big job, but TOGETHER, they can do it. Teamwork - here we come!

Thanks so much for your love and support, guyssss!

Please let me know in the comments below if you're able to help me make this a successful launch, and feel free to tag others you think might be interested in this fun little read."

Keep it short, engaging, and fun. Note that I included the fact that it's a children's book, and mentioned the target age group, the topic, and that it's a short read. I also asked my friends and family to tag others who might be interested in this topic, so be sure to post it as a "public" post.

Adding an image of your book's cover can also help create buzz and excitement, and will help make your post stand out even more. And don't forget to directly tag people you think might be interested, especially if they have little ones who fall within your targeted age group.

Make it as easy as possible for people to help you. You will want to provide those who agree to help with a free ebook version of your book before you publish it, so they have enough time to read it. As you won't know which format each person prefers, it's beneficial to create a file that holds multiple formats (e.g., .epub, .mobi, .pdf).

REVIEWS

As you want everyone on your team to leave a review as soon as you publish your book, it helps to make the review writing process as easy as possible. For example, you can let them know that a review of one or two sentences is sufficient. Tell them how crucial early reviews are for the success of your book, and remind them what an important role each member of your team is playing.

To go above and beyond, you could provide your launch team with a set of review structures that will help get them started with the review. This is something I learned from publicity strategist and expert Selena Soo. For example, you could prompt them with sentence structures such as these, to get their wheels turning:

- "As a [YOUR PROFESSION], I really found chapter [#] so helpful, because [XYZ]."
- "I love the story that [AUTHOR] shared in chapter [#] about [XYZ], because [ABC]."

As you provide them with all this information, do try to be respectful of your launch team's time and keep your emails to them as short and concise as possible.

HOW TO ENSURE THAT YOU KEEP EVERY SINGLE REVIEW

Reviewers need to follow a set of rules to ensure their review is approved by and remains on Amazon, and you need to make your launch team aware of these. We don't know for certain to what extent these factors play a role, but to mitigate the loss of any reviews, I suggest you stick to these.

1. **UNTRACEABLE URL:**

   When sending your launch team the Amazon link for your book, or when sharing the link on social media, make sure you use a "clean" URL. What do I mean by that? When you're searching for a book on Amazon, Amazon will add a "tail" to the searched book's URL, adding information such as the search terms used. It also adds what account made this search. If you share this link with all this information attached, Amazon can tell that it comes from you, the author. And that's something we do not want. It doesn't necessarily mean that whoever uses that URL to purchase your book will have their review removed, but why take the risk?

   Below is a search I performed for author Otakara Klettke's children's book *Detective Bella Unleashed*. The first link includes all sorts of information, such as my used search terms and account-specific information. Cutting out that additional information will leave us with the book's title and the Amazon Standard Identification Number (ASIN) or 10-digit ISBN. To cut the URL down even further, you can take out the book's title completely, only leaving the ASIN (or 10-digit ISBN). Using this stripped-down link will make it untraceable. And that's the link you should share.

   ① https://www.amazon.com/Case-Missing-Detective-Bella-Unleashed/dp/0997907037/ref=asap_bc?ie=UTF8

   ② https://www.amazon.com/Case-Missing-Detective-Bella-Unleashed/dp/0997907037

③ https://www.amazon.com/dp/0997907037

2. VERIFIED REVIEWS:

Once you have launched your book, ask your launch team members to download the book directly from Amazon, even if they already received a free version from you before the launch. Doing so will make their submitted review a verified purchase review. Verified purchase reviews are important because they are an important metric on Amazon. You'll also notice that verified reviews always show up before any un-verified reviews.

Word of caution: Ask your launch team not to use their Kindle Unlimited subscription when downloading your book, because doing so will leave their review as an un-verified review.

A super book for the young and the young at heart.
October 31, 2017
Format: Kindle Edition   Verified Purchase

3. READ BOOK AT LEAST PARTIALLY:

Make sure to let your team members know that they have to at least partially read the book they just downloaded before submitting a review. As they will already have read the pre-launch file you sent, they might skip this step, so be sure to tell them how important this is. Even if they just page through it on their e-reading device, it's important, as Amazon is able to tell whether or not the reviewer actually looked at and spent any time within the book files.

4. **WAITING PERIOD:**

    Make sure to let your team members know not to post a review right after they purchased the book, but rather to wait at least a couple of hours. It's best to page through parts of the book, close it, and return to it at a later time to place the review.

5. **CONNECTIONS:**

    Make sure to let your team members know that the review shouldn't identify the reviewer as an acquaintance, family member, or someone who knows the author, as this may disqualify the launch team member from leaving a review.

Encourage people on your launch team to post on social media that they left a review. Doing so might make others in their circle of friends curious, plus it gives you the chance to thank them publicly for supporting you and your book.

Every review is so very important. To ensure that all submitted reviews are accepted and will remain on Amazon, I have created a ➘ *Book Review Guide* that you can send to your launch team members. Step by step, it lets them know how exactly to leave a review, and includes all the valuable information we just covered.

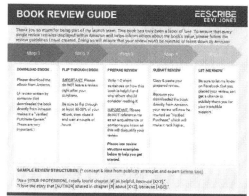

➘ [http://www.eevijones.com/book-downloads]

WHAT ABOUT REVIEWS THAT GET DELETED ANYWAYS?

Amazon keeps a very watchful eye on authors' reviews. So what if reviews get deleted even after your readers followed all the steps outlined above?

If that should happen, then you can always post that particular review within your book description site's "Editorial Reviews" section. This section is generally reserved for public or official reviews, such as from Kirkus, an established American book review magazine, but you can add any reviews you'd like.

If you decide to do so, I'd suggest to add the reviewer's professional title as well, to make it look more qualified. For children's books, professions such as Kindergarten Teacher, Teacher, Librarian or the like are relevant to your audience and can therefore be highly effective when highlighted within this section.

Now that we have covered why forming a launch team is so important to a successful launch, and have talked about all the intricacies involved when asking for properly and carefully placed reviews, we can shift our attention to promoting our book.

PROMOTIONS

Promotion plays an important role in your launch – it encompasses the ways in which you are going to be spreading the word about your new book. You will be implementing various promotional strategies, focusing on the most important and effective ones.

Be aware that there are many ways to go about this. Just google 'book promotion' and you'll receive thousands upon thousands of search results. It's very easy to be pulled into this rabbit hole of trying this method here and another over there. But we all have limited time to devote to this task. And that's why I'm going to show you the most time-effective methods for successfully spreading the word about your new children's book, so that it can reach as many people as possible.

Up until now, we have been in pre-launch mode, the period *after* setting up on Createspace and KDP, but *before* the actual publishing of the book. To move on, I'd like to go over the terms I'll be using post-launch.

To prevent confusion throughout this marketing section, I'll use a different term for each launch segment. To visualize this, I've created a timeline graph for our ↘ *Launch Segment Sequence.* You can find the PDF among the book downloads.

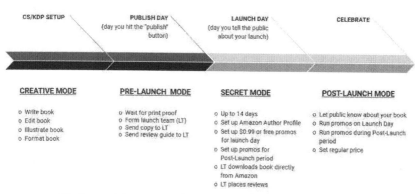

↘ [http://www.eevijones.com/book-downloads]

Publishing day is the day when we hit the submit button within Createspace and KDP. Be aware that once you hit this button, it can take up to 72 hours for your book to actually appear on Amazon and be available for purchase, although this usually happens a lot sooner.

Go ahead and hit the publish button for both your paperback and ebook. This will begin our "secret mode."

Paperback and ebook will link together automatically after a couple of days. If they don't, you can call either Createspace or KDP. Just make sure that you claim both paperback and ebook in Amazon Author

Central before you call them (see below on how and where to set up an Author Central account).

Remember how I told you paperbacks are still outselling ebooks for children's books? The ebook version of your children's book is really only important for promotional purposes. Firstly, it's an inexpensive way for your launch team to purchase your book so that they can leave a verified review, and secondly it enables you to place your book on promotional sites that require your book to either be free or $0.99.

The ultimate goal, however, is for people to discover your book, and to like it so much that they decide to purchase the paperback version for their children. Once you have a good number of reviews as social proof, people will be much more likely to pay higher prices for the paperback.

Whenever I hold a promotion for one of my ebooks, for example, sales spike for its paperback version as well.

Once your book appears within Amazon's marketplace, you can go ahead and set your promotional pricing for your ebook, if you haven't already done so. Most authors choose a price between $0 and $0.99. By now, you should have decided whether or not you would like to give KDP Select a go in order to be able to offer your book for free for up to five days. Remember that if you decide to do so, you won't be able to upload your ebook onto any other platforms – even your own website – for 90 days.

Now is the time to let your launch team know they should download your book directly from Amazon, either for free or for $0.99, depending on whether or not you decided to go with KDP Select. Either way, make sure they download it from Amazon in order to make their reviews fall under the "verified purchase" category. Make sure they have the ⭘ *Launch Team Review Guide* I provided you with earlier, to ensure that all reviews remain on Amazon.

Remember, you're still in "secret mode," so make sure your launch team members don't share any of this yet.

The following are marketing strategies you can set up to get as much as possible out of your book's launch. You might not be able to try them all; just pick those you think will work best for you.

1. AUTHOR PROFILE

Now that your book is live, you'll want to set up your author profile so it's ready when your book appears on Amazon. Your author profile is where your potential reader can learn more about you. This is the page that people land on when they click on your name as displayed right next to the cover of your book's Amazon page.

At the very least, add a polished bio, a head and shoulders photograph, and a link to your website. All the information you include can be edited any time.

To set up your profile, go to https://authorcentral.amazon.com. Upon joining, you will be able to add your new book to your account, as well as promotional book trailers, a link to your website, a short bio, photos, and much more.

If you were to click on my name next to one of my books, you would see a screen similar to the screenshot below. Your equivalent page will hold your book (once you've added it), and any other information you decide to add. For example, I have added book trailers for each of my books.

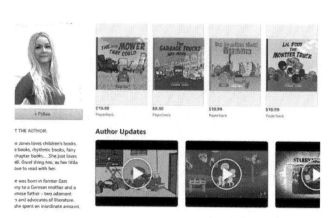

2. PROMOTIONAL SITES

To encourage people to download your book, you will have to set up a number of promotions. These can either be paid or completely free. Be aware that some sites require you to offer your book for free in order for them to run your promotion, so you won't be able to use those if you didn't opt into KDP Select.

There are many sites that allow you to post about your book promotions. Some require you to submit the promotional dates up to two weeks in advance, while others allow listings with less than 24-hours' notice.

As you have to enter your book's Amazon URL during the booking process, you can only do so after you have published it. The goal is to set up a number of promotions during the "secret mode," so that the sites can give your book some momentum with Amazon's algorithm.

In order to make this as easy as possible for you, without having to sift through hundreds of lists, I've created one that holds ➘ *Promotional Sites* that offer children's book-specific genres.

You will find that some are free, and some require a fee; some require your book to be free, and some allow a reduced price. You decide what best suits your budget. Also notice that some of these sites require you to already have a certain number of reviews before they promote your book – another reason why having a launch team is so very important.

By now, you should already have a number of reviews from members of your launch team. Keep encouraging your team to leave a review for your book.

Set up your promotions so that some will run during the "secret mode," and some after you officially announce your book, during the "post-launch mode."

Launch day is the day you officially announce your book to the world. Now is the time to ask your launch team to share news of your book on social media. To make it as easy as possible for your team members to spread the word, you could create images for them to share on their social platforms, such as Facebook and Twitter.

Make sure to publish your post and the image as "public" so it can be freely shared. Have a clear call to action either in the image itself or in the post accompanying it, so people looking at the image know exactly what to do next. And don't forget to include the "cleaned" Amazon link to your book.

Above are two examples of how to go about this. Author Sarah Mazor, for example, chose to display her book cover with the added text "Kindle Edition – FREE – Today." And author Melinda Kinsman showcases all of her books, along with her website. With a free graphic design tool like Canva (https://www.canva.com), you can create an image like these in no time at all.

3. FRIENDS & FAMILY

Don't forget about your own friends and family. Now that you have officially launched your book, you could create or take an appealing image of your new book and post something like this:

Make sure to include the "cleaned" link to your Amazon page, and that your status is set to "public" so your friends and family can share it.

Depending on which platforms you're active on, you can announce your new children's book on Instagram, Twitter, Pinterest, and even LinkedIn.

RELEVANT HASHTAGS:

#BoardBooks
#BookMarketing
#ChildrensBooks
#EarlyReaders
#IndieAuthors
#KidLit
#KidLitArt
#KidsBooks
#Kindle
#KindleDeals
#MustRead
#PictureBook
#ReadYourWorld

(If you have a specific subject in your book, be sure to check for hashtags that relate to it; e.g., #monkeys, ...)

You can also email friends and family who aren't on social media. This is a great way to reach extended networks, such as old coworkers, high school friends, and distant cousins.

Consider offering gift copies while your book is still at $0.99. To do so, go to your book's Amazon page and click "Give As A Gift." You'll be charged $0.99, but you'll receive 35% back as royalties. You can send reminders of the gift later, should someone forget to download the book. An additional benefit is that these gifted copies count toward your ranking within Amazon – but the sale won't count until the book is downloaded, and the desired review won't take place unless they read the book, so be prepared to remind them.

Always be sure to be specific with your asks. Ask for downloads, and always ask for reviews.

4. FACEBOOK GROUPS

Joining audience-specific Facebook groups is absolutely free and can be very beneficial. Facebook groups and pages are a great place to display and promote your newly published children's book. You can inform members about your sales, giveaways, and other promotions. This is the place where parents come to find the next read for their children and where authors support each other. Just make sure to be mindful of others and only post according to each group's administrative rules.

You will be able to use the same images you created above.

As before, I've created a list of ➘ *Facebook Groups* relevant to our genre. Go ahead and click through, and see which ones you'd like to join in order to participate and promote.

As well as groups from my list, be sure to dig into the potential your book's topic brings with it. If, for example, you have written a book about beautiful mermaids, go ahead and look for Facebook groups formed around this particular interest. Make sure to ask for the admin's permission to post your book as a comment. This can be a very powerful method, as every member of that group is potentially your target audience.

Launch teams, promotional sites, and Facebook groups are mainly used during the "secret mode" and up to two weeks immediately following your launch day and public announcement. We'll now look at a number of promotional methods that can be implemented during the weeks following this initial launch period. As you will see, promoting your book is a continuous effort, as you try to give it as much exposure as possible.

By now, your book's price will have returned to its previous set price, if you used KDP Select. If you wish to slightly increase your current price, now would be a good time to do so. As discussed during the uploading and pricing section in the previous chapter, be sure to set your price in such a way that it remains competitive with books similar to yours.

5. GOODREADS GIVEAWAY

Goodreads (https://www.goodreads.com) is an enormous social platform centered around books. It was acquired by Amazon a number of years ago. Users can add books to their personal bookshelves, rate and review books, and get suggestions for future reading choices based on their reviews of previously read books. It is an excellent resource, helping booklovers find books they might want to read.

I recommend using this platform to host a giveaway – I have done so for each of my books. You can list any of your pre-released or published books for a giveaway, regardless of publication date, as long as a paperback version is available.

After setting up a Goodreads account, you will be able to set up an author account. And once you do that, you can list a giveaway.

Goodreads suggests you run your giveaway for as long as a month. I usually host mine for about two weeks only, mainly because you'll see the number of entries spikes at the beginning, when the giveaway is new, and at the end, just before it finishes. These are the times your giveaway is being "pushed" by Goodreads. There isn't much activity in between, so stretching it out doesn't really have any additional benefits.

Goodreads also recommends offering at least 10 books, reasoning that at least 60 percent of giveaway winners review books they win. I know this sounds promising, but this hasn't been true for me, as in my case very few winners actually ended up posting a review. And if they did, they posted the review on Goodreads only.

We don't use Goodreads only to get reviews, though. The main reason we're hosting a giveaway is to increase our exposure. To illustrate, my four most recent giveaways have had an average of 1439 entries. Most of these entrants added my book to their "to read" shelf, and each time a giveaway ended, I saw a spike in sales, meaning some of those who entered but didn't win ended up purchasing my book. So this is what we're really trying to get out of this giveaway.

Most recent giveaways

Lil Foot The Monster Truck

1309 people requested it
status: approved
ends: June 14, 2017 11:59PM

The Monster Numbers Book

1323 people requested it
status: approved
ends: December 17, 2016 11:59PM

The Garbage Trucks Are Here

1974 people requested it
status: approved
ends: December 16, 2016 11:59PM

The Little Mower That Could

1148 people requested it
status: approved
ends: September 26, 2016 11:59PM

When setting up your giveaway, it's important to have a catchy little description. This description will have to address how many copies you're giving away. If you're planning to sign your copies, mention that as well, as it will add to the perceived value.

I usually write something like this:

Enter for a chance to win 1 of 2 SIGNED copies of the newly released "The Amulet Of Amser: The Case of the Mona Lisa."

AGES 7-12

Wen's very first fantasy adventure in the middle-grade chapter book series – The Amulet of Amser: The Case of the Mona Lisa.

Blending history with fiction, children learn about famous pieces of art. Wen, the youngest member of the Amser family, is destined by his family's ancient oath to forever protect the world's most precious pieces of art for all of mankind. During a visit to his grandfather's house, Wen learns that he can influence what will happen tomorrow by going back in time. Will Wen be able to save the Mona Lisa, or will Leonardo da Vinci's masterpiece be lost forever?

More THE AMULET OF AMSER books:
"The Case Of The Starry Night"

To learn more and to watch the BOOK TRAILER, visit www.Yvonne-Jones.com

When setting up your giveaway, you get to select which countries will be able to participate. As I'm sending signed copies directly from my home, I usually select USA and Canada only, mainly because of the shipping costs.

It's best to set up your giveaway at least seven to ten days in advance, to allow for approval and any last-minute edits.

6. CHILDREN'S BOOK AWARDS

An award-winning book will bring increased recognition and provides critical acclaim, helping to make your marketing journey much easier.

There are numerous awards for self-published children's books. Most charge an entry fee, ranging from $50 per title to $500+, but winning one of these competitions and being able to display the winning seal will help set your book apart. I've compiled a list of the best and most reputable ↘ *Awards* for the children's book genre. Be aware that some of these require you to send in one or more paperbacks of your book.

The dates and prices I include reflect the early bird pricing. The earlier you enter your book, the more cost effective it will be.

7. CHILDREN'S BOOK FESTIVALS

Book fairs are a great way to get the word out about your book, as they give you the chance to directly interact with your target audience. I've put together an international ↘ *List of Children's-Book-Specific Festivals*, including the month in which each is held, so you can prepare and apply in advance. A paperback version of your book is a must for this promotional option.

8. GUEST POSTING / MAGAZINE ARTICLES

Guest posting (or *guest blogging*) means to write and publish an article on someone else's website, blog, or in a magazine. Guest posting is a great strategy, as it directly targets your ideal audience. It is, however, somewhat more time consuming, because you not only have to find the right blogs or magazines to approach, you also have to write a valuable and insightful article in order for it to attract new potential readers.

Here is an example – this is an article I wrote for *Indie Authors Monthly* (*I.A.M.*, https://www.indieauthorsmonthly.com), a magazine that aims to connect readers with new authors while being the go-to source for indie author news, processes and events. With more than 2 million views per month, it's a great way to get your name out there.

And here is an article in the magazine *Exceptional Parent* (http://www.eparent.com), in which I was interviewed by Hope Arvanitis, an award-winning communications professional.

You can go about your article-writing and pitching in two different ways:

a. TARGETED APPROACH:

Approach blogs that cater to people who already love the topic of your children's book. For example, if your book is about Monster Trucks, approach a blog that already writes about Monster Trucks. Ask yourself, would this particular audience be interested in reading about what you have to say? If the answer is yes, the blogger is more likely to allow you to guest post for him or her.

b. GENERAL APPROACH:

Approach more general blogs that cater to parents with children your target age. For example, if your book is for 2–5-year-olds, it would make sense to approach sites such as *Scary Mommy*, which has an entire section dedicated to articles written for parents of children this age.

When it comes to guest posting, be aware that your post can't be a sales pitch. Your written piece will have to be about something relevant to that particular blog's audience, tied to your book in a natural and non-pushy way.

When searching for a suitable blog or site to pitch a post to, start with what you know already. What family sites are you reading? What parenting/ mom blogs are you enjoying? What sites are you subscribed to? Go to these sites and see if they welcome guest bloggers. And if they do, approach them, offer a giveaway for their readers, and let them know your idea for a post. If they like it, they'll agree to post it and share it with their audience. If they don't, either come back with a different idea to pitch or move on to another site.

If you want to expand your search, make use of the many lists that already exist online. For example, if you're looking for family-related blogs, type "Best 100 Family Blogs" into your search engine. If your children's book is about dogs, type in something like "Top 100 Dog Blogs." If you have never pitched an article before, approach blogs further down that list first. As a blog that's still up and coming, they'll be more likely to accept pitches from a new author.

This will require some trial and error, but can spread your book's message in so many ways.

To get you started, I have created a ⬎ *List of Blogs* that accept submissions for children's books. Make sure to check out each site in order to determine whether or not your book would be a good fit.

9. SCHOOL VISITS

Many children's book authors don't realize that many schools set aside an annual budget for paid author visits. School visits can be either free or paid – I suggest offering free visits for your first couple of times.

Send an email to your nearby schools and offer to do a reading of your book. Be sure to say what age range the book is aimed at, so that the administration can choose age-appropriate classes. Send an image of your cover, and include a short synopsis, links to your reviews on Amazon, and to your website, if you have one.

Make sure to follow up the email with a phone call to let them know that you visit local schools for free, in return for the school sending slips home, offering the chance to buy signed copies of the book.

If the school agrees, offer to send a summary of your planned visit. The more control you have over this process, the more likely you are to get the sales. If you're travelling farther, you'll need to work out travel time and costs, and decide whether you wish to charge a fee.

10. PODCASTING

Just like guest posting, podcasting can be a very powerful way to spread the word about your book far and wide. There are many family- and kids-related podcasts that host interviews. You can use the same technique I introduced above, and search for "Top 100 Family Podcasts," or any other topic that relates to your children's book. In addition to a search on Google, you can use iTunes to find the best and most popular podcasts in any given category.

This example is award-winning children's book author Carol P. Roman's podcast *Let's Say Hello To Our Neighbors*. During this interview, I was able to talk about my books and upcoming projects. Interviews like this provide you with a great opportunity to connect with many listeners and to spread your message.

[http://www.blogtalkradio.com/storytellers-campfire/2017/07/25/lets-say-show-hello-to-our-neighbors-radio-show]

As podcasts are becoming more and more popular, there might even be someone among your friends or family who hosts one, who would love to have you as a guest.

And don't forget, you don't just have to talk about your book. You can talk about your experience of writing the book and the story behind it. Why did you write this particular book? How did you go about it? These are all questions people ask me over and over again, so use your journey to becoming an author to pitch yourself to these podcasts.

11. JOIN SCBWI

If you plan on writing more than one children's book, I'd suggest you join SCBWI.

The Society of Children's Book Writers and Illustrators (SCBWI) is an extensive network of writers, illustrators, editors, publishers, agents, librarians, educators, booksellers, and others involved with literature for young people. It provides education and support for these individuals through awards, grants, programs, and events.

With more than 22,000 members worldwide, it is the largest children's writing organization in the world. SCBWI is membership-based. Your first year of membership is $95; thereafter the annual renewal fee is $80.

I have been a member for multiple years now, and find its resources helpful and the community very involved and supportive.

To learn more, visit http://www.scbwi.org.

12. BOOK TRAILERS

Being able to reach readers directly is the holy grail for authors of children's books. Of course, the number one place we can do this is during school visits and book fairs. But what about online?

Nowadays, children are all over YouTube. Between 35% and 45% of UK children aged 4–7 visit YouTube each week. From age 8 upwards, that jumps to 60%, increasing to around 80% by age 11 (Source: Egmont/Nielsen 2015 Children's Deep Dive study).

A Smarty Pants "brand popularity" survey of 6–12 year-olds in the USA found that YouTube beat the likes of Disney, Netflix for Kids, Nickelodeon, and Lego.

And that's where the use of book trailers comes in.

I mentioned earlier that I like having book trailers for my children's books. This is definitely optional, and is really just for fun and little ones' entertainment. My sons love watching these trailers.

Book trailers can be a wonderful addition to your marketing strategy. You can use them in places such as your newsletters, Facebook, Instagram, Goodreads, Amazon Author Page, YouTube, and your own website. These mini videos generate more buzz in social networks and engage new audiences in an exciting way. Book trailers may be a fairly new concept, but they truly work when done well.

Below is the trailer for my book *The Impatient Little Vacuum*, created by my own Book Trailer Production Studio. If you should decide to have a trailer created for your children's book, I've included a number of book trailer producers at the end of this chapter. As before, make sure the producer you're planning to hire has a number of trailers specifically for children's books within their portfolio.

[https://www.youtube.com/watch?v=SgCXBEfvg9o]

As you've probably noticed, some of these methods of promotion are more suitable for long-term marketing. Promoting your book is an ongoing process.

BONUS: ASKING INFLUENCERS FOR REVIEWS

One of my favorite strategies is the influencer marketing strategy. This may take some time to bear fruit, but is very powerful when done correctly.

Influencers are individuals who have influence over potential buyers. Sometimes it makes sense to ask an influencer to provide an editorial review for you.

Years ago, when I contacted my very first influencer, I'd never heard of "influencer marketing." I didn't even know that this was considered a marketing technique. I just did it because I felt this insatiable urge to spread my books' messages.

Receiving a review from an influencer can lend enormous credibility to your book. If he or she agrees to do a review, it's very likely they will also promote or mention your book to their audience. This is an excellent promotional strategy and really works if done correctly. I have used this strategy on three of my books.

"This book contributes greatly to the public's understanding of our military members and their families."
~ Ike Skelton, Former U.S. Representative

"This resource is perfect for EVERYONE with ANY connection to the military community, and should be on everyone's shelf!"
~ Judy Davis, TheDirectionDiva.com

"Hip, Hip Hooray! Teeny Totty is the BEST at showing how to use the BIG Potty!"
~ Teri Crane, Bestselling Author of *Potty Train Your Child In Just One Day*

"Throughout the book, there are constant reminders that trying something new is fun. And good. And brave. And how being a Big Kid feels awesome."
~ Jamie Glowacki, CEO and Author of *Oh Crap! Potty Training*

"Lil Foot is a mightly little truck with a mighty big heart."
~ Bob Chandler, Creator of *Bigfoot*, the original Monster Truck

Notice that my books' topics were relevant to each influencer I approached.

As the former chairman of the House Armed Services Committee, late honorable U.S. Representative Ike Skelton was the perfect person to talk to about my very first book (nonfiction), *Closing the Gap: Understanding Your Service(wo)man.*

I also contacted Judy Davis from TheDirectionDiva, as she is a military spouse well known within the military community, and very engaged when it comes to the well-being of military families.

For my very first children's book, *Teeny Totty Uses Mama's Big Potty*, I contacted Jamie Glowackie, the go-to guru when it comes to potty training toddlers, and published author of *Oh Crap! Potty Training*. As an expert in the field of potty training, I really wanted to connect with her, as I felt her audience would benefit from my book as well.

Speaker, author, and consultant Teri Crane is nationally known as the Potty Pro to thousands of parents, teachers and childcare providers. She has appeared and been featured in media including *Good Morning America*, CNN, NPR, *Publisher's Weekly*, *Parents*, *Parenting*, and *Men's Health*. As the bestselling author of *Potty Train Your Child in Just ONE Day: Proven Secrets of the Potty Pro*, I was beyond excited when she agreed to review my book.

One of my latest books, *Lil Foot The Monster Truck*, made use of the trademarked name *Bigfoot*, and I therefore had to ask for permission to use this name in my story. This provided the perfect segue to asking the owner and founder of the original monster truck, Bob Chandler, to review my book as well.

To see a sample of how I contacted these influencers, I've included the ➘ *Original Influencer Email* I sent to Jamie Glowackie.

It's important to be genuine about your interest in the influencers' work. Only contact them if you have been following them for at least a little while, and only if you truly value their work. Don't contact them purely for your own sake – try to bring actual value to the influencers' audiences as well. Ask yourself whether or not their audience would benefit from learning about your mission or your book, and only go forward if the answer is "yes."

Be sure to thank the influencer once you receive your review. Bob Chandler, the creator of the original Big Foot and founder of the Monster Truck sport, for example, received a bouquet of flowers along with a thank-you note after I published *Lil Foot The Monster Truck*.

Getting these reviews may take some time. You can either approach the influencer before your book is published, or after you already have an actual paperback in hand. I took the latter approach, as I wanted to be able to send out a paperback if it was requested.

Once you receive an editorial review, you can place it directly onto your book's cover, and on Amazon under the "Editorial Review" section.

Teen Totty Uses Mama's Big Potty,

Editorial Reviews - Back Cover

Closing The Gap: Understanding Your Service(wo)man,

Editorial Reviews - Back Cover

YOUR TO DOs FOR THIS CHAPTER:

- ☐ Form a launch team
- ☐ Set up an Amazon author profile
- ☐ Set up promotions
- ☐ Hit the "publish" button
- ☐ Promote your book

Be sure to use all the lists, templates, and swipe files I've provided you with. You can find them here:

↘ http://www.eevijones.com/book-downloads

FEATURED BOOK MARKETING SERVICES

Below is a list of marketing services and other resource providers that I have either previously worked with or have had recommended to me by other authors. I've presented them in alphabetical order.

Please note that I am not an affiliate to any of these services. I'm not being compensated by any of these artists or service providers in any way. It's just my way of showing my appreciation for such an amazing community and is meant to spread the word about and among truly amazing people.

(* these are my own services)

MARKETING RESOURCES:

SCHOOL VISIT EXPERTS (Find advice on how to create and deliver quality author visit programs for kids, teachers and librarians)
http://schoolvisitexperts.com

MARKETING SERVICES

AUTHOR BUZZ (Get smart multi-platform buzz for your book)
http://www.authorbuzz.com/kids

AWAY WE GO MEDIA – JULIE GERBER (Social Media Management)
https://www.awaywegomedia.com

CHILDREN'S BOOK REVIEW (A wonderful author showcase area with a range of interview options)
https://www.thechildrensbookreview.com

MAX BOOK PR (A PR firm specializing in the promotion of authors and their books)
http://maxbookpr.com

MARKETING STRATEGISTS

ASHLEY EMMA (Author marketing services)
http://ashleyemmaauthor.com/author-marketing-services

* EESCRIBE (Helps aspiring children's book authors to write, illustrate, format, and publish their first children's book)
http://eescribe.com

ERIC VAN DER HOPE (Book marketing coach)
http://ericvanderhope.com

GABRIELA CASINEANU (Book promotion and author marketing)
http://www.gabrielacasineanu.com/for-authors

MEGAN WAGNER (Marketing creative agency)
https://www.mwmarcom.com

BOOK TRAILER PRODUCERS

* LOEWENHERZ-CREATIVE STUDIO
http://loewenherz-creative.com

STICKVIDEOS (Creates kinetic typography animated videos)
https://www.fiverr.com/stickvideos

WINDING OAK
http://windingoak.com

CHAPTER NINE

NOW IT'S YOUR TURN

You are *so* meant to write this beautiful children's book of yours! Do you recall your *WHY*, which we determined at the beginning of this journey? Let your very own, unique *WHY* motivate you throughout this creative process of writing your book.

Remember, 81% of Americans want to write a book, and you're one of the very, very few who are taking actual steps toward achieving this goal.

My intention for this book was to provide both a comprehensive strategy and loads of motivation to implement these concepts. I've shared with you the exact same methods I use when writing, illustrating, publishing, and marketing my own children's books.

I've shared the insights, steps and processes that took me years to figure out, so you can implement them in weeks, instead of years. You should now have everything you need to create your very own children's book.

But remember, you have to take action. These steps and insights mean nothing if you don't implement them.

If you want more help, I can offer two additional resources:

1. Sign up to get my insights and guides at http://eevijones.com. If you have found the concepts and ideas in this book motivating and helpful, follow me as I continue to learn, grow, and share additional lessons along the way.
2. If you want to write your children's book with even more support and accountability, feel free to view my different Coaching Programs, during which I will guide you through each step of the process, one on one.

I know that these methods will work for you. I have helped aspiring authors from all walks of life, from lawyers, neuroscientists, clinical psychologists, and filmmakers, all the way to moms, dads, and grandparents, at all stages of their writing careers.

If you picked up this book, I know you have what it takes to make your dream of writing a children's book a reality. You have what it takes to make your dream come true.

Find all the swipe files and templates I created for you here: www.eevijones.com/book-downloads.

I truly hope this book provides you with everything you need to make your dream of writing a children's book a reality. I can't wait to see you succeed. Once you hit the publish button, I would love to hear from you and learn about your book. You can contact me at hello@eevijones.com. I read every message I receive.

Always remember, the number one thing that will set you apart is taking action.

~ E.

REQUEST

THANK YOU FOR READING MY BOOK!

It would mean the world to me if you could take a short minute to leave a review on Amazon, as your kind feedback is much appreciated and so very important.

http://eevijones.com/amazon

Thank you so very much for your time!

~ E.

INSIDER TIPS
INSIDER TIPS FROM SUCCESSFUL CHILDREN'S BOOK AUTHORS

I love tooting other authors' horns. And to show you the vast and colorful world of self-published children's books, I've spoken to a number of successful self-published children's book authors, and asked them what they believe to be the most valuable piece of advice to give to aspiring children's book authors. What do they wish they'd known before they worked on their first children's book?

I've presented all authors in alphabetical order.

CAROLE P. ROMAN

Carole is an award-winning children's book author, and has penned more than 40 books.

Carole's most valuable insider tip for aspiring children's book authors:

"Writing a book may feel like a solitary experience. It's not. Get on an author-driven Goodreads thread and talk to other writers. I never fail to learn something new, and when I'm not sure about something, there are so many people who can offer both inspiration and guidance making the journey less lonely and more successful."

You can find her wonderful work here:
https://www.amazon.com/Carole-P.-Roman/e/B008ZOXI0W
http://caroleproman.com

DANNY BLITZ (Author)
&
SHERIDAN BLITZ (Illustrator, Co-Author)

"Much to Do Before a Dog" is Danny's first children's picture book in collaboration with her 17-year old daughter as the illustrator and co-author.

Danny's most valuable insight for aspiring children's book authors:

"Write and illustrate an age-appropriate book. You must know the developmental markers to be successful with this. Test your book on your audience, preferably in person before you publish to get honest feedback, both said and unsaid, from the children and their adult readers."

You can find her beautiful work here:
http://www.amazon.com/much-to-do-before-a-dog/dp/B0741RXSLB
https://www.mamacat.org/much-to-do-before-a-dog

NATALIE McNEE

Natalie is an international best-selling ghostwriter, but nothing brings her more joy than creating children's picture books and novels.

Natalie's most valuable insight for aspiring children's book authors:

"Don't get too attached to your words or story. Creating a book is a collaboration between critique partners, editors, proofreaders, illustrators, cover designers and beta readers. Almost all will suggest changes. It may seem like it's no longer your story after the changes are made but it will be the best story for your readers."

You can find her beautiful work here:
https://www.amazon.com/Natalie-McNee/e/B07789C8CS
https://nataliemcneebooks.com

OTAKARA KLETTKE

Otakara Klettke is an international bestselling author and the creator of the children's book series Detective Bella Unleashed - tales told from a dog's unique perspective.

Otakara's most valuable insight for aspiring children's book authors:

"If you're doing a series, make sure you can book the same illustrator for the next book."

You can find her adorable work here:
https://www.amazon.com/Otakara-Klettke/e/B01KGNPTDS

PETER THOMAS

Peter is the bestselling author and creator of the Adventures of Billy Bee children's book series.

Peter's most valuable insight for aspiring children's book authors:

"Make sure your story is good!!! Make sure it interests the children! Make sure it captivates them! The children are the most truthful audience anyone can ever go in front of. Test your work with them before you go spending hundreds and even thousands of dollars on your project. Schools are always looking for activities for the children. If you approach the PTA or PTO of any school or know of any teachers or even students you can make the connections you need to get in front of the children and you'll know right away if there are any areas that need work or if you're ready to go to print!!!"

You can find his wonderful work here:
https://www.amazon.com/Peter-Thomas/e/B01N2XQJ2J
http://areallygreatstory.com

WENDY VAN DE POLL
MS, CEOL

Wendy is the author of The Adventures of Ms. Addie Pants, a timeless picture book series about one hopeful little puppy and a strong little girl who teach each other about love, friendship, and trust.

Wendy's most valuable insight for aspiring children's book authors:

"My best advice for any aspiring children's book author is to gather a knowledgeable team. Writing is the fun and the creative part. But it can be stressful when you first start out with all the backend tasks needing to get done. The best way to reduce that stress is to be sure to have an editor and a formatter that knows the business. Make sure they have vast experience, great testimonials, and can solve problems that come up with ease. There is a huge learning curve for a self-published author and it doesn't need to be unnecessarily difficult. Your experience will be more enjoyable with a great team and a great team will allow you to flow in your creative process."

You can find her incredible work here:
https://www.amazon.com/Wendy-Van-de-Poll/e/B01BMUWX7O
https://wendyvandepoll.com

LIST OF SWIPE FILES
& TEMPLATES

To access all the templates and swipe files I have created for you, visit
http://www.eevijones.com/book-downloads.

Make sure to bookmark this page for easy access and reference.

1. My WHY Sheet
2. Children's Book Roadmap
3. Idea Sheet
4. 300 Things Children Like
5. Structure Sheet
6. Chapter Book Formula
7. Editor Email Template
8. Illustrator Project Description
9. Sample Illustration Request
10. Illustrator Brief
11. Art Release Form
12. Children's Book Fonts
13. Launch Team Book Review Guide
14. Launch Plan
15. Marketing Your Children's Book – Promotional Sites
16. Marketing Your Children's Book – Facebook Groups
17. Marketing Your Children's Book – Book Awards
18. Marketing Your Children's Book – Festivals
19. List of Blogs Reviewing Children's Books
20. Influencer Email

RESOURCES

Here is the list of resources I have referred to throughout the book. Please note that I am not an affiliate to any of these sites or programs, except where noted. I'm just passing on what brought great value to my own writing process.

(* these are my own services)

BARCODE GENERATOR
http://bookow.com/resources.php

BOWKER
https://www.myidentifiers.com

CALIBRE
https://calibre-ebook.com/download

CANVA
https://www.canva.com

CREATESPACE
https://www.createspace.com

*EESCRIBE
http://eescribe.com

FIVERR
http://fiverr.com

FREELANCER
http://freelancer.com

GENIUS SCAN (app that takes pictures, like a scanner)
https://www.thegrizzlylabs.com/genius-scan

IDIOMS & SLANG RESOURCE
http://www.englishdaily626.com/idioms.php

INCHES-TO-PIXELS CONVERTER
https://www.ninjaunits.com/converters/pixels/inches-pixels

KDP KIDS BOOK CREATOR
https://kdp.amazon.com/en_US/kids

KINDLEPRENEUR DESCRIPTION GENERATOR
https://kindlepreneur.com/amazon-book-description-generator

*LOEWENHERZ-CREATIVE
http://loewenherz-creative.com

NIELSEN
https://www.Nielsen.com

ONE LOOK DICTIONARY
http://www.onelook.com

PIXELS-TO-INCHES CONVERTER
https://www.ninjaunits.com/converters/pixels/pixels-inches

RHYME ZONE
http://rhymezone.com

SCRIVENER (a word-processing program and outliner designed for authors): http://www.literatureandlatte.com/scrivener.php

SELF-PUBLISHING SCHOOL (affiliate link):
https://xe172.isrefer.com/go/sps4fta-vts/bookbrosinc3405

SIGIL
https://www.techspot.com/downloads/5797-sigil.html

SIMPLIFY YOUR WORDS & PHRASES
http://www.plainlanguage.gov/howto/wordsuggestions/simplewords.cfm

SLANG DICTIONARY
http://onlineslangdictionary.com/word-list/0-a

SLIDESHARE
https://www.slideshare.net

STORY CLOSINGS
http://www.folktale.net/endings.html

STORY OPENINGS
http://www.folktale.net/openers.html

SURVEY MONKEY
https://www.surveymonkey.com

THESAURUS
http://www.thesaurus.com

UPWORK
https://www.upwork.com

US CENSUS
https://www.census.gov

VELLUM
https://vellum.pub

WRITTEN SOUND DICTIONARY (Onomatopoeia Dictionary)
http://www.writtensound.com/index.php

REFERENCED BOOKS
REFERENCED BOOKS IN THE TEXT

━━━◆◆●◆◆━━━

A Gemstone Adventure – by Yvonne Jones
Amelia Bedelia – by Peggy Parish
Closing The Deal On Your Terms – by Kristine Kathryn Rusch
Closing The Gap: Understanding Your Service(wo)man – by Yvonne Jones
Colors in Hebrew – by Sarah Mazor
Detective Bella Unleashed – by Otakara Klettke
Good Night, Gorilla – by Peggy Rathmann
How Authors Sell Publishing Rights – by Helen Sedwick & Orna Ross
Jamberry – by Bruce Degen
Knuffle Bunny – by Mo Willems
Lil Foot The Monster Truck – by Yvonne Jones
Ocean Commotion – by Janeen Mason
Self-Publisher's Legal Handbook – by Helen Sedwick
The Amulet of Amser – The Case Of the Mona Lisa – by Yvonne Jones
The Amulet of Amser – The Case Of the Starry Night – by Yvonne Jones
The Garbage Trucks Are Here – by Yvonne Jones
The Impatient Little Vacuum – by Yvonne Jones
The Little Mower That Could – by Yvonne Jones
The Magic Tree House – by Mary Pope Osborne

REQUEST

THANK YOU FOR READING MY BOOK!

It would mean the world to me if you could take a short minute to leave a review on Amazon, as your kind feedback is much appreciated and so very important.

http://eevijones.com/amazon

Thank you so very much for your time!

~ E.

ABOUT THE AUTHOR

Y. Eevi is the bestselling author of more than a dozen children's books. She loves children's books – picture books, rhythmic books, fairy tales, chapter books… Eevi just loves them all. Good thing too, as her little ones love to read with her.

She's the founder of EEscribe, an online resource for aspiring children's book authors. Through EEscribe, she has helped many people on their journey to writing and publishing their first children's book.

She has been featured in multiple media outlets, such as TEDx, Scary Mommy, Kindlepreneur, Huffington Post, EP Magazine, Military.com, and Stars & Stripes.

Eevi currently lives on the East Coast with her husband and their two sons. In theory, she is working on her next children's book. In reality, she is probably being tickled or busy pretend-playing with her little ones.

She can be found online at http://www.eevijones.com.

Made in the USA
Columbia, SC
07 February 2024

31678459R00098